ABOUT JADE

Jade Hameister began her Polar Hat-Trick quest in April 2016 at the age of 14, when she became the youngest person in history to ski to the North Pole from anywhere outside the last degree and was awarded Australian Geographic Society's Young Adventurer of the Year as a result. In June 2017, she became the youngest woman to complete the 550-kilometre crossing of Greenland, the second largest ice cap on the planet unsupported and unassisted. In January 2018, Jade skied 600 kilometres from the coast of Antarctica to the South Pole unsupported and unassisted, after an epic 37-day journey via a new route through the Transantarctic Mountains and up the Kansas Glacier, from the Amundsen Coast.

In finishing this incredible journey, Jade has set a number of world records, including:

- the youngest person to ski from the coast of Antarctica to the South Pole unsupported and unassisted
- the first Australian woman in history to ski from the coast to the South Pole unsupported and unassisted
- the first woman to set a new route to the South Pole unsupported and unassisted
- the youngest person to ski to both Poles
- the youngest person to complete the Polar Hat-Trick.

In 2018, she was recognised by *Vogue* magazine as one of the year's Game Changers, was awarded one of ten Women of Style awards by *InStyle* magazine, alongside Elle Macpherson and Delta Goodrem, and spoke on behalf of Oceania at the Opening Ceremony of Pope Francis' International Climate Change Conference at the Vatican.

Jade lives in Melbourne and is currently a year 11 student.

'What an extraordinary adventure Jade is on! When people say it cannot be done, think of Jade and you will realise that anything is possible with bloody hard work, single-minded focus, courage and determination. Well done, Jade, you are a true inspiration.'

JANINE ALLIS, founder of Boost Juice

'Jade is a remarkable young woman in every sense of the word. Not only is she achieving things no one else like her ever has, she is determined to shift the focus from what we look like to what we do. In a world that tells everyone, but particularly young women, that their value is in their appearance, Jade's kick-butt, can-do attitude and record-breaking achievements are a welcome breath of fresh air. She is a role-model to many, and rightly so!'

DR SUSAN CARLAND, academic and author

'Congratulations, Jade! Against such extreme conditions amongst a big, beautiful dream, we can all see your determination and we are so happy for what you are doing for young people all around the world. Xx'

EMMA WATKINS, Wiggle

'Jade Hameister is courage personified. What an awesome achievement.'

JAMILA RIZVI, author, presenter
and political commentator

'What an incredible achievement by Jade. She has proven that age is no barrier, her tenacity is something we can all admire and learn from. It takes a very strong-willed person to set themselves a challenge like this and to then see it through, despite all the physical and emotional obstacles. Jade is a remarkable role model for women everywhere. I can't wait to see what she does next! Congratulations!'

JESSICA SMITH, Paralympian

JADE HAMEISTER
MY POLAR DREAM

JADE HAMEISTER
MY POLAR DREAM

MACMILLAN
Pan Macmillan Australia

First published 2018 in Macmillan by Pan Macmillan Australia Pty Ltd
1 Market Street, Sydney, New South Wales, Australia, 2000

Cataloguing-in-Publication entry is available
from the National Library of Australia
http://catalogue.nla.gov.au

Typeset in 12.5/18 pt Bembo by Midland Typesetters, Australia
Printed by McPherson's Printing Group
The TEDx talk on page 67 used with kind permission from TEDxMelbourne.

The author and the publisher have made every effort to contact copyright holders
for material used in this book. Any person or organisation that may have been
overlooked should contact the publisher.

To my beautiful family, Paul, Vanessa,
and Kane, for supporting my dreams.

The past couple of years have been filled with crazy new experiences — experiences that have transformed me and my soul. New pins on my map, new smells, new tastes, new friends, new cultures and a new mindset. I've pushed myself past what I once thought were my boundaries and challenged what other people once thought was possible for young women. I've set world records, been to places where no human has ever set foot before and fully immersed myself in the here and now of each new challenge. I've chased moments that I can't explain. Moments with emotions and adrenaline highs, where I felt on top of the world or in the depths of despair. Moments that can't ever be replicated or relived. I've constantly been in good company and surrounded myself with humans who make me a better version of the person I was yesterday. A lot of people tell me I'm crazy and ask me why I would do something so insane. But I think the real question is, why would I not do something I'm so insane about? I think you're crazy not to chase your wildest dreams. Crazy to live a safe life with no risk and to not do the things that set your soul on fire. The best stories are the unexpected, unplanned ones. This constant passion and fire inside of me that drives me to want to explore and experience the unknown is my why. These are the things I live for. The moments that make me feel alive. Thank you for allowing me to share my journeys with you.

Jade x

CONTENTS

PROLOGUE
THAT SANDWICH

For the last three years, I have dedicated my spare time to achieving my dream of the Polar Hat-Trick – skiing to the North Pole, crossing Greenland coast to coast and skiing from the coast of Antarctica to the South Pole.

When I'd returned home from reaching the North Pole, at 14 years old, TEDx approached me with the opportunity to deliver a talk discussing a 'big idea worth sharing'. It was a life-changing experience and I was a combination of excited and nervous.

My TEDx talk – which was about trying to shift the focus for young women from how we appear to the possibilities of what we can do – was then uploaded to YouTube so that it was free for anyone around the world to watch. It was incredible to have this platform to share a message so important to me with so many young people, but what I hadn't really wrapped my head around was the possible online trolling in response to my talk. The majority of responses it received were of support and encouragement, but there were some negative comments, too – most of them demeaning to women.

Make me a sandwich.

Good on you, sweetie. Maybe you could find a successful husband and make him a sandwich.

Sorry little lady – you were designed to be a homemaker, have babies and take care of them. Not to trot around in snow to prove a point. ACCEPT YOUR ROLE AND PLAY IT.

Make me a sandwich.

Every time someone posted a positive comment, these trolls would respond with: 'Make me a sandwich.'

My first reaction was just to laugh, but deep down I was also kind of annoyed. The people who make these sexist comments and bully online are doing it, usually anonymously, from behind the safety of a keyboard. Not only are they insecure, but they're dinosaurs – the world has moved on and they've been left behind.

Later, when we were on our way to the South Pole, occasionally we would joke about these comments on my talk. When we finally arrived at the Pole we spent the day cleaning out our sleds and getting ready for our flight back to Union Glacier the next morning. Dad was pretty tired, so after dinner he went back to our tent to call Mum and I stayed up with the rest of the team and a few other adventurers watching *Back to the Future*. It was then that I decided to carry out a joke – make a sandwich and walk the kilometre from camp back to the Pole and take a photo to post to my Instagram account. Heath and Ming also agreed to come with me and take the photo.

It was around 11 pm when I went back to the tent to tell Dad what we were planning to do (it is 24-hour daylight in Antarctica in summer, so there were no issues there). He told me it was a stupid idea, and that I should just zip myself into my sleeping bag and get some recovery rest. When I told him I was going to do it anyway, he asked me not to wake him up when I got back in the tent.

I posted the photo that night along with the words, '. . . for all those men who commented "make me a sandwich" on my TEDx talk . . . I made you a sandwich (ham & cheese), now ski 37 days and 600 km to the South Pole and you can eat it xx'.

At the time, I had about 3000 Instagram followers and I only wanted to take the sandwich picture mainly for a bit of a laugh. Obviously, there was a message behind it to the men who'd made the comments, but I hadn't really analysed it in that way, and I was pretty sure none of them followed me on social media, so they would never see the photo to get my message anyway – it was more symbolic.

But around the time we got back home to Australia, the social media site AJ+ had already made a video telling my story and picked up the sandwich photo. It was viewed more than five million times and things just snowballed from there.

Within a few weeks, I had more than 12,000 Instagram followers and there were media enquiries coming in from all over the world. I was spending more time on Skype doing interviews than I was catching up on my homework. I felt there was a lot of pressure and, in some cases, I was being labelled a feminist icon.

But I'm not sure that's what I am or want to be. For me, it's about equality. I've been brought up in a family where the fact that I am female has never entered any discussion about what is possible. There is no 'us and them' in my mind. We absolutely need to empower women around the world, but everyone, both male and female, should benefit from that empowerment. We all need to work together as one human race to make our world a better place.

All the stories that followed also stirred up thousands of online comments. Lots of men responded that I was just being a compliant female and doing what I was told to do — I went and made that sandwich.

The truth is, I didn't. I asked the camp's male chef, Michel, if he could make me a sandwich to take to the Pole for the photo, and he did.

So the joke was on the dinosaurs, again.

Me and Michel, the French chef at the South Pole
camp, who made me that sandwich.

HOW IT ALL BEGAN

1
BORN TO BE BRAVE

My parents have always said that they believe I was born a fighter.

I arrived into this world at the Royal Women's Hospital in Melbourne on 5 June 2001, and as far as anyone could tell, I was a healthy baby girl. But three days later, and for no apparent reason, I stopped breathing.

I was in my crib in Mum's hospital room. Dad was there and one of Mum's friends was visiting. Dad looked over and saw that my face had turned purple. He didn't say anything to Mum, but calmly picked me up, took me over to the nurses' station and asked if they thought there was a problem. The movement must have made me breathe again, because when the nurses looked at me, there was nothing wrong.

Dad took me back to Mum's room and put me in the crib. He said nothing to Mum and her friend, but he didn't take his eyes off me.

Within the hour, I went purple again. Again, he picked me up and took me to the nurses. This time, I didn't resume breathing.

The nurses hit the code-blue alarm, and medical staff ran from everywhere to try to resuscitate me. They then rushed me off to the special care unit – and Mum and Dad's nightmare began.

Mum had heard the commotion outside her room, but she had no idea that I was the cause of all the fuss until Dad asked her friend to leave, then explained to Mum what had happened. Mum has told me since that when it happened, she felt her heart stop. Her brain froze and she doesn't remember when it started working again. Instead of being in my crib beside her, I was now in the care of others and all Mum was left with were questions. What was wrong with me? Was I going to survive? Would I have brain damage from lack of oxygen? She was terrified.

To make matters worse, there were no answers. I would unexpectedly stop breathing – sometimes half-a-dozen times a day or more. Mum was discharged and sent home without me (Dad said she was a wreck) while I remained at the hospital with an army of doctors and specialists running tests, trying to work out what was going on.

Mum would return to spend all day at the hospital with me while Dad was at work, then Dad would sit by my crib all night. They were determined to watch over me every minute, so that if something went wrong they could make sure I got the attention I needed. Dad would read me stories through the night. He says his favourite was *The Lion King*, except he made Simba a lioness. As he watched over me, so small and helpless, he promised me that, if I lived, he would do anything in his power to help me achieve my dreams.

After two long weeks, the doctors still didn't know what was causing me to stop breathing. Eventually, when I'd gone a couple of days in a row without an episode, I was allowed to go home. Like most parents, Mum and Dad were excited the day had come, but also extremely anxious. They were taught how to perform CPR on a newborn and were provided with a breathing monitor and plenty of good wishes.

The breathing monitor was connected by sticky tape to the place where my umbilical cord had been. When I stopped breathing, an alarm would go off and that's when Mum and Dad were supposed to start the CPR – though the doctor told them that if it got to the point where I needed CPR, it was probably too late anyway . . . I'm sure that was reassuring.

Mum was so worried about being alone with me in case something should happen that Dad decided to take a year off work so he could be there with us. Mum told me later that it was the worst of times, but also the best. She and Dad worked together as a team and it made their marriage stronger than ever.

After seven or so months, my breathing problems cleared up. I had proven to be a survivor. I have no doubt that this beginning altered something in my chemistry.

✳

Some of my earliest memories are of Dad going off on adventures. He began climbing big peaks in 2007. He'd also had a couple of near-death experiences in his life – one when he was just seven years old and was hit in the head by a tyre rolling fast down a steep hill, resulting in a multiple-fracture exploded skull. These experiences led him to believe he should never take life for granted. He was constantly reminding me and my younger brother, Kane, of this when we were little – and he still does!

His taste for adventure and exploration has taken him from surfing three-metre swells on newly formed breaks in Indonesia's remote Banda Aceh shortly after the 2004 earthquake and tsunami, to an extended whitewater rafting expedition in Nepal. He's even walked the Kokoda Track twice – once with his dad and again with Kane when he was thirteen. And earlier this year, Dad and Kane covered around 1000 kilometres exploring remote and unexplored parts of the Amazon jungle with Matsés tribesmen as their guides and Peru Special Forces escorts.

When I was about five years old, Dad decided he'd like to climb Mount Aconcagua in the Andes. Aconcagua is the second-highest of the Seven Summits (the tallest mountain on each of the seven continents) and the highest peak in the Southern Hemisphere.

He was one of only three of his party of 11 to reach the peak on that expedition. A man in the group ahead of Dad's team died from altitude sickness and one of the guys Dad reached the summit with fell on the way down and knocked himself unconscious, which made for a very slow descent in bad weather. Off the back of this climb, Mum and Dad raised $20,000 to purchase new breathing monitors for the Royal Children's Hospital.

Dad went on to climb Mont Blanc (completing a climb that normally takes five days in less than 24 hours), Kilimanjaro in Africa, Russia's Mount Elbrus, Vinson in Antarctica, Denali in Alaska and, of course, Mount Everest. He reached the top of Everest in 2011. By 2013, he was the twelfth Australian to have completed the Seven Summits.

In 2008, the whole family climbed Mount Kosciuszko. I was six years old at the time and Kane was just four. It felt great to be at lunch during primary school and able to say we had climbed the highest mountain in Australia on our holidays, though in reality it's not very extreme! From an early age, adventure was just a regular part of our family life. Dad would come home laden with photographs and stories, and Kane and I thought taking on massive challenges and pushing boundaries was just a normal way to live.

2
BIG DREAMS

At the age of 12, I somehow convinced the rest of the family to go to Nepal and hike to Everest Base Camp together. Base Camp is 5400 metres above sea level and it takes 12 days to get there. The summit of Mount Everest is 8848 metres above sea level and was first climbed by Sir Edmund Hillary and Tenzing Norgay in 1953. I'd heard a lot of Dad's stories about climbing Everest and I really wanted to be a part of that world and see the places I had only created the image of in my mind.

Climbing the tallest mountain in the world was never going to be possible for our whole family at the ages of 12 and 10, but trekking to Base Camp was still an incredibly exciting adventure. It was such a magical part of the world to spend time in. Dad arranged for us to trek with a team that included some of his old expedition friends who would continue on in an attempt to summit Mount Everest. Each day we trekked through villages, met some of the beautiful local people and spent the evening playing cards with the sherpas and mingling with other travellers. I can honestly say that the experience changed my life. It made me think about what I could potentially achieve as a young woman in the world of adventure and exploration.

One of the members of our group who was going on to climb to the top of Everest was Vilborg Arna Gissurardóttir – or Villa, as we called her. Villa is from Iceland and she had already skied solo from the coast of Antarctica to the South Pole and had also crossed the Greenland ice cap. As we walked during the day, Villa would share stories with me about her expeditions and answer any and all of my questions. I'm sure I got pretty annoying at times, since she was trying to focus on her attempt at summitting the highest mountain on the planet, but she was very generous with her time and I will be forever in her debt. She had an incredible 'anything is possible' kind of vibe. All her adventures sounded so crazy – but so crazy awesome.

Villa didn't make it to the top of Everest on that trip – there was an avalanche in the Khumbu Icefall and the season was shut down before anyone could attempt a summit. She returned the following year and was caught in the avalanche at Base Camp caused by the terrible earthquake in Nepal. Again, the season was cancelled. But she didn't give up. In 2017 she became the first Icelandic woman to make it to the top of Everest.

Villa's words of encouragement on my trek to Everest Base Camp stayed with me, and after we arrived home I began to create my own ideas of adventures in my imagination.

When I was in year seven, I decided to run for middle school captain. It was my big goal that year and I had my heart set on it. However, I didn't get chosen, but my best friend did. While I was incredibly proud of my friend (and she did an amazing job in the role), I was also quietly really upset at the time. It seems like such a small thing now, but it fired me up and made me determined to find something else to work towards – something that was important to me but which wasn't related to school. Adventure was second nature to me so that was where my focus naturally turned. I decided I wanted to ski to the South Pole, just like Villa had done.

I mentioned the idea to Dad first, and the two of us agreed we should do some more research into it as I really had no idea what I was asking for. Dad spoke to an expedition company he had used many times before, and they assured him it was possible to ski to the South Pole at 14 years of age if one was properly prepared. Armed with that knowledge, we sat down with Mum and Kane and told them what I wanted to attempt to do.

Mum and Dad were, in principle, in support, but with the condition that Dad would have to go with me given my age.

But before I was given the go-ahead, Dad said I had to prove that this was something I was really passionate about and committed to doing. He devised a rigorous training program and my goal was to stick to it. I didn't miss a session.

But life in the suburbs of Melbourne hadn't exactly given me the skills I'd need to ski for weeks on end while dragging a sled in some of the coldest parts of the world. In fact, I had never really skiied before – however, I was willing and excited to learn.

Dad and I organised a trip to New Zealand so we could both learn how to cross-country ski at a place called Snow Farm. Honestly, I hated it at first. I loved the snow, but I felt incredibly uncoordinated the first time I put on skis, and my muscles ached in ways I never expected. I remember watching the experienced skiers and feeling so out of place, but for some reason that only motivated me more.

We then flew by helicopter to the Tasman Glacier in the middle of one of New Zealand's coldest winters. There, Dean Staples – a good friend of Dad's, who had been his guide on Everest (Dean has summitted Everest nine times) – taught me all sorts of polar expedition skills. Dad wanted to see if this really was something I was going to enjoy. He told me later that he'd half expected me to say it was a lot harder than I'd thought it would be, and to give up on the journey to the South Pole.

In temperatures as low as –20°C, I learned to walk on icy slopes in crampons, harness a huge sled to myself and, wearing skis, drag it across the snow for hours. I also learned how to get myself out of a crevasse. Crevasses are dark, seemingly bottomless cracks in the ice that are mostly hidden beneath thin layers of snow. Falling into a crevasse was one of my greatest fears from the beginning; I knew I'd have to learn how to deal with it myself if that was to happen, though, and I was dreading it.

After teaching me some theory and showing me how to tie various knots, Dean created an anchor at the top edge of the biggest crevasse we could find and lowered me in. I was then left in mid-air, dangling off the side of a crevasse in the middle of nowhere. I had to use two small loops of rope called prusiks, which were attached to the main safety rope on my harness, to slowly inch my way up the ice wall to the ground above me.

Dad walked away at this point. He told me later that it wasn't because he didn't care, but because he knew it was going to be really difficult and frustrating and I needed to find a way to work through it on my own.

It took me almost an hour to get out. I was in tears and shaking the whole time. My hands were numb and aching from the cold. I kept creating scenarios in my head where the rope would snap or the anchor would break loose. I felt like giving up multiple times and yelling to Dean to just lift me out, but I couldn't let myself; I made it out on my own and when I reached the surface, I received the most incredible thrill.

I was hooked.

Everything we did during our time in New Zealand was completely new to me, but it made me really hyped for the future. I was ready to train hard and do anything else necessary to get to the South Pole at the end of the year.

Back in Melbourne, while we were driving to the gym for another gruelling training session one day, Dad hit me with some bad news. He'd received a phone call from the owner of the expedition company we were going to use for my South Pole trip. The logistics company in Antarctica had advised them they wouldn't allow me to ski to the South Pole at the age of 14 – it was a long-standing rule that the company would not support expeditions for anyone under sixteen. Dad told me he had tried everything he could think of to find a way around it, but their decision was final.

I was gutted. I'd already done so much preparation. Fortunately, we'd kept my plans very secret, so I didn't have to explain to everyone what had happened and could work through my hurt without a thousand questions.

After feeling sorry for myself for a few days, I decided I wasn't going to let this setback wreck my dream. With Mum and Dad's encouragement, I began to consider what other trips I might be able to do before I turned 16 to help me prepare for Antarctica.

After a lot of research, I came up with a new plan for us. First, I would like to ski to the North Pole, which I could do at 14, but at this early stage I hadn't really considered or understood the decisions that needed to be made around starting points for this trip. Then I would like to try to cross Greenland, the second-largest ice cap on the planet. This was a common preparatory expedition for a full-length South Pole trip, so it seemed to make sense before I headed to Antarctica. And if I managed to complete all three expeditions, I would have achieved what is known as the Big Three polar expeditions, or the 'Polar Hat-Trick'.

I now had a new polar dream, and it proved to me once again that everything happens for a reason – that setbacks can be transformed into opportunities.

Having revised my goals, we only had about nine months in which to try to put all the pieces in place to make the North Pole a reality. The North Pole expedition season starts in April each year and it's short – there are only a few weeks when it's considered safe to attempt the journey.

To start with, we needed a guide.

After a few emails and phone calls, we found Eric Philips, the first Australian to ski to the North and South Poles. He had been guiding polar expeditions for 25 years, lived in Tasmania and owned a company called Ice Trek. Eric flew to Melbourne to meet me and get comfortable that a 14-year-old would be up to the task. He signed up to be our guide on the expedition.

We then needed to confirm funding for the expedition.

When Dad had summitted Everest, he and Dean, who was also a cinematographer, had filmed their journey. The resulting documentary, *Everest: The Promise*, was distributed by a Melbourne film production company, WTFN, and it aired on the Discovery Channel. Dad mentioned my quest to complete the Polar Hat-Trick to the CEO of WTFN, Daryl Talbot, and Daryl asked if I would be interested in allowing a cameraperson to accompany me on my journey. WTFN then took the idea to a few different organisations they thought would be interested in helping with finance and logistics, and National Geographic said yes, and made a significant financial commitment.

Having the financial support of Nat Geo was unbelievable, but, looking back now, I realise that the money was the least valuable piece of my partnership with them – it opened up so many new opportunities for me. I am so grateful to have had such an incredible organisation involved with my journeys.

For the following months, getting to the North Pole was my focus. I would go to school and continue to do everything a normal 14-year-old would do, but I was also planning to ski more than 150 kilometres over a new and harsh environment. I had to get used to juggling the two worlds I now lived in.

Dad and I would go the gym four or five times a week to work on strength training, plus we'd do another two sessions to improve our aerobic conditioning. That could involve anything from dragging tyres on the beach using a harness (the closest we could get to pulling a sled on snow) to hours of stair climbs. Each of these sessions lasted anything from 90 minutes to two hours and they were as much about pushing on when you felt like giving up as they were about building fitness. As physically strong as I needed to be to take on this expedition, it was going to be the mental side that would really test my limits.

THE
NORTH
POLE

EXPEDITION 1

Destination: The North Pole

Distance: A 150-kilometre journey from outside the last degree, starting at 88'40

Duration: 11 days, May 2016

Goal: To be the youngest person in history to make the trip

Team: Me, Dad, guide Eric Philips, cameraman Petter Nyquist

Big challenges: Dad's kidney stone, delays from cracks in the ice runway, danger of falling into the freezing Arctic Ocean, open water leads, compression zones, polar bears, a race to beat the end of the season

Everyday challenges: Skiing, homesickness, wondering if Dad was okay

3
FALSE STARTS AND MIDNIGHT EMERGENCIES

Just when you think everything is going to plan, things can change in an instant.

For more than a year I'd been training hard to tackle my first polar expedition. I was feeling physically ready for the North Pole trip, but I had some concerns too.

I remember one specific night at the gym, where I had a major episode of self-doubt and fear. I wondered just what we thought we were doing even attempting this expedition. Here I was, a 14-year-old girl from Melbourne who had barely even seen snow, attempting to set a world record on skis. Who did I think I was?

I was also starting to dwell on the dangers we could encounter along the way. There was the real possibility of plunging through the thin floating sea ice on which we would be travelling, into the freezing Arctic Ocean below. There were also polar bears, who can smell humans from up to 20 kilometres away and have been known to stalk polar adventurers for days. But because the actual trip still seemed like a dream, these hazards did too.

The night before we were due to fly to Oslo and then on to Svalbard, Dad and I went through all of our gear one more time, just to make sure we weren't leaving anything behind and that everything was working as it should be. All that was left to do was pack it all into our bags. To keep things calm and at least semi-normal, Kane and I decided to play a game of cards after Mum had dished up one of Dad's and my last home-cooked meal for a while. Dad told us he didn't feel very well and he went up to bed early.

I'd only been asleep for about an hour when I woke to the sound of Dad's voice.

'I'm going to go downstairs to sleep, so I don't keep you awake,' he said to Mum.

It was only about half an hour later when I woke again. This time the voices were louder, more anxious.

'Do you want me to call an ambulance?' Mum asked.

What? Ambulance!

I went downstairs to find Dad doubled over in pain on the floor. He'd been busy all week with work and organising the final details for the trip, and had been ignoring some abdominal issues. But this was bad – I could tell immediately from the grimace on his face.

Mum called emergency services, but when the ambulance hadn't turned up 20 minutes later, Dad decided he was going to drive himself to the hospital even though he was in excruciating pain. Mum was trying to help him, but he kept saying he could look after himself.

The situation quickly became very chaotic. We had no idea what was wrong with Dad and he was starting to make less sense as his pain intensified. What if Dad was seriously ill? What if we had to abandon everything we'd worked towards?

The next morning, Mum told me that Dad had a large kidney stone and would soon be going into surgery – the day of our departure – to have it removed. I was almost convinced that our big adventure was going to be over before it even began. But Dad being Dad, he'd told Mum before he went into surgery that he was going to get on the flight, even though the surgeon was strongly recommending that he shouldn't travel so soon after his operation.

I tried to believe it was possible, even though as the hours ticked away, we had no news from the hospital. I fought hard to keep in the flow as if everything was proceeding as normal. Thankfully the day was full of distractions – a blur of interviews and filming with National Geographic. I didn't love having a camera shoved in my face to capture my raw emotions, but my polar journey was now being filmed for a documentary, so it was necessary. My two best friends Zoe and Mia came over after school to say goodbye and it all became very real.

Dad arrived home from hospital at 6 pm – after only waking up from his general anaesthetic at around 4 pm! He was very groggy and we worked together to finalise the packing and zip up our bags. Our taxi was picking us up at 7 pm to head to the airport, so we ate a rushed meal together and said our final farewells. It was obvious Mum was more than a little worried.

The travel was incredibly long. Melbourne to Dubai was a 14-hour flight, and from there, another seven-hour flight to Oslo. We then had a nine-hour stopover before the final leg of just over two and a half hours of flying to Longyearbyen in Svalbard. I spent most of the journey worrying about Dad. He now had a plastic stent between his kidney and bladder to help him pee – unfortunately he was peeing lots of blood – and his forearm was bleeding from the hole left behind when a nurse had pulled the IV drip out in the car park. (He'd left the hospital in such a hurry the nurses forgot to remove it, and he was halfway home before he realised and had to turn around. A nurse met him in the car park to take it out.) He was wearing special circulation socks on the plane to stop the blood from clotting after the surgery, and seeing them kept reminding me of what had just happened.

Eric met us at the airport in Longyearbyen and checked us into the hotel, where we called Mum and Kane before falling asleep.

The next day, Eric (who was staying across town) was due to pick us up at midday to explore a bit of the town. I sat in the hotel foyer writing in my diary and admiring the unique landscape out the window. I became more and more nervous. It was so cold outside and I knew it would be about 20 times colder out on the ice – and we were going to be out there for the next couple of weeks.

I was already homesick and missing Mum and Kane like crazy. Mum sent me a thought to consider over the coming days, and it really rang true: 'If I quit now, I will soon be back where I started. And where I started I was desperately wishing to be where I am now.'

I knew right then that if I decided to quit, I'd regret it forever. I had to keep at it.

I knew this in my heart, but my head was still loud with doubt.

Longyearbyen is the largest town in Svalbard, Norway – though with a population of about 2500 people it's not really large at all. It started out as a coal-mining town in the early 1900s, but these days it's the centre of the tourism industry for the Arctic. Cruise ships leave from here to explore the fjords, icebergs and wildlife of the ice-bound north and it's where anyone like us, preparing to ski to the North Pole, does their final preparations. The town consists of heaps of colourful houses and buildings, a few shops, some restaurants, a bar and a museum. Not that we had much time to explore. Our second day was all about making the final preparations before heading off.

We were doing this journey 'unsupported and unassisted' – that was our plan for all three expeditions. These are technical terms used in the adventure community to help classify expeditions. 'Unsupported' means no support is received via using dogs, kites, vehicles, etc. – you can only use human power to progress. 'Unassisted' means that you carry all your needs in your own sled – you cannot receive any resupplies along the journey, either by way of air drop or depots. Unsupported and unassisted is obviously the hardest way to undertake these expeditions, but also the purest – that's what appealed to me – the risk of failure would be higher, but the feeling of achievement would be so much greater if we could pull it off.

Amongst the contents of our sled was all our food rations. Breakfast would be Eric's 'breakfast bomb' (protein powder, powdered milk and pecans and shredded coconut for flavour). Lunch would consist of a chunk of salami and a chunk of cheese, a packet of two-minute noodles and a few dried biscuits, but I'd never eat everything because my hands would get too cold and eventually be too painful to function. Dinner would be dehydrated packeted meals and Dad and I'd share a double serve in the tent at night. We'd also have a hot drink in the morning (chai latte) and a hot drink at night (Milo). We needed to eat about three times as many calories as we normally would to ensure we had enough energy. The only thing we wouldn't be carrying was water. We'd be travelling across ice, so there'd be no shortage of it to melt. The only issue was that, because the ice we'd be moving across was frozen sea, it might be hard to find water that wasn't slightly salty. The older the sea ice, the less salt it contains. In multi-year ice, nearly all the salt has drained away and it makes fresh water that is fine for drinking when melted – such ice is a different colour and not too hard to identify with a bit of coaching.

Eric showed us how to pack the sleds for while we were out on the ice. Everything we needed during the day had to be placed at the front of the sled, because the last thing you'd want to be doing is unzipping and unpacking the sled to find something while your body is very quickly cooling down as you've stopped moving. We didn't know what the weather would be like, and we needed to prepare for the worst.

We first met our cameraman, Petter Nyquist, in Longyearbyen too. I became really good friends with him over the course of the expedition. This North Pole expedition was my first experience with the camera in my face and I hated it to start with, but after becoming quite close with Petter, I would just pretend as though I was having a conversation with a friend when he asked me questions on camera. He was the perfect personality for a novice like me – Petter was patient, funny and really cared about how I was feeling. He would prove to be an expert skier and the hardest-working member of our expedition. Petter carried all the camera equipment himself in his sled – the camera people for Greenland and the South Pole would have an assistant to drag these heavier loads.

That night, we had dinner with two other teams that were also undertaking expeditions to the North Pole. There were incredible people on our table, and they were all experienced adventurers with so many stories.

Colin O'Brady was at the dinner and was aiming to do the Seven Summits and the two Poles in five months – otherwise known as the Explorers' Grand Slam. He completed this feat when he reached the peak of Denali in Alaska on 27 May 2016, nearly two months after we met. He set a speed record of 139 days, which was 58 days faster than the previous record holder. This was made even more amazing by the fact that Colin had suffered second- and third-degree burns to 25 per cent of his body during an accident in Thailand at the beginning of 2008. He'd had multiple operations and, at one point, doctors thought he may never be able to walk properly again.

Then I met Dixie Dansercoer, one of the world's most renowned polar explorers, who had completed land to land crossings at both Poles. He has achieved some extraordinary feats: he was the first to trek from Siberia to Greenland in 2007 and completed the first full circumnavigation of the Greenland ice cap in 2014. Dixie never explores just for the sake of adventure, though. All his expeditions also incorporate a scientific element, which I think is really cool.

Audun Tholfsen was there as well. He had skied and kayaked from the North Pole to his home town of Longyear-byen in 2012. The journey took more than two months, and he received the Shackleton Award, which honours outstanding expedition achievements, for his efforts.

It certainly felt weird being the only female, not to mention the only 14-year-old, among these inspiring people. They had so many stories to tell, while my story was just beginning.

❄

During our third day in Svalbard we got out on the ice to test our systems, pulling our sleds behind us for four hours to replicate the conditions we'd encounter over the next couple of weeks. I could see that Dad, still fresh from surgery, found this tough going, but he assured me he was fine. Eric also showed us how to set up the camp and light the gas stoves. The tents were a lot bigger than I'd imagined, which was a bit of a relief since Dad and I were going to be sharing one. We'd be spending every moment of the next two weeks together, and although we were really close, being in such a confined space with anyone for so long was going to be a challenge. I knew we'd be pushed to physical extremes and I'd trained myself as hard as I could for that, but how I would cope with the emotional and psychological part of this journey, I was unsure.

I was made even more unsure when the bad news continued to roll on in. Victor Serov, the key liaison person for operations at the Barneo camp, arrived in Svalbard. Barneo is the Russian camp built each year on the sea ice, from where North Pole expeditions depart. He was there to tell the various teams that were preparing for the trip that the runway built on the floating sea ice had cracked in a couple of places. One of the fissures was 30 centimetres wide and the other 20 centimetres. He and his team were searching for a new ice floe on which to construct another runway, but he estimated that would take about a week. In fact, all the expeditions that had been booked were being reconsidered. Someone suggested that instead of the last two degrees of latitude, we just do a single degree, which is the last 112 kilometres to the Pole, in order to make sure we get there in time before the season is over. As much as I wanted to make it to the Pole in time, the double degree, 224 kilometres, was always the first plan and I wasn't interested in taking the easy way out.

Eric was adamant this setback wouldn't affect us at all – that the Russians would work out some way to get the season back on track. During all this craziness, I also found out that the plane that took people to Barneo last year had crashed after the landing gear failed. Luckily, no one died.

The delay of a few days meant we were going to miss some really cold weather, with temperatures dropping to below −40°C around the Pole. As we waited, I caught up on some schoolwork. I was missing a few weeks of school to do this trip and I knew there would be a bit to catch up on when I got home. It also took my mind off the broken runway for a while. Dad was very relaxed about the delay. He saw it as a chance to slowly rebuild his strength post-surgery.

Later, we were alerted that another crack had opened up on the runway. You get yourself so hyped up and ready to go and then – boom! – something goes wrong and there's another change of plans. By now, it was starting to become draining and, for me, quite upsetting. But I had to remind myself that everything happens for a reason, and avoid getting upset about things that were out of my control.

While it seemed that nothing was going according to plan, it was still overwhelming to be in such a unique environment. To fill in the time, Dad and I went on a few mini adventures. We went dog sledding and ice caving, took a cruise to an old Russian town, and practised pulling our sleds and getting used to our skis, considering we were both still very uncoordinated. So, while the delays were a disappointment, Longyearbyen had provided me with some of the greatest experiences of my life so far and I would definitely be back.

A week later, the Russians still hadn't managed to create a new runway. Eric and the other polar guides were told there might not be any expeditions at all to the North Pole that year. This was unprecedented and really opened my eyes to the changing climate, which I would have otherwise been oblivious to. If the season had been cancelled completely, I would have been devastated. When Eric briefed us that this was a real possibility, it was an emotional low point, especially for a 14-year-old who didn't know better.

The North Pole Marathon, which is run in multiple laps around a short course at Barneo (not at the North Pole), was supposed to start at about the same time as our expedition, so the whole town was full of competitors, all of them waiting for their flight onto the sea ice and trying to shuffle around hotels as their check-out dates came and went with no departure for Barneo. We were all wandering around in a state of limbo.

Just when I'd almost convinced myself we'd be heading back to Melbourne without even beginning, the Russians managed to finish building their fourth runway this season. Overnight, no less! We were told we'd be on the first flight to Barneo, departing at midnight, with the other longer-distance North Pole expedition teams.

Finally, we were packing our sleds for real and on our way to the airport.

SOME COOL FACTS ABOUT...

The North Pole

- The Geographic North Pole, the goal of our expedition, is the northernmost point on the planet and is the top of the axis on which Earth is spinning. It's a fixed point and is diametrically opposite to the Geographic South Pole.

- The location of the Magnetic North Pole changes daily based on the planet's magnetic field. When you use a compass, it points to the Magnetic North Pole, not the Geographic North Pole.

- The North Pole is located in the middle of the Arctic Ocean on a massive ice floe, a floating piece of Arctic sea ice, that can shrink to half its size in the summer.

- The nearest land is about 800 kilometres away.

- An expedition from land to the North Pole is considered almost impossible these days, given the extent of sea-ice melt from global warming.

- On 4 May 1990, Børge Ousland and Erling Kagge reached the North Pole on skis without resupply, after a journey lasting 58 days, making them the first people to reach the North Pole from land unsupported.

- The Soviet Union built the first North Pole ice station, about 20 kilometres from the actual North Pole, in 1937. Four men conducted scientific research for the following 274 days before they were collected by an ice breaker ship. By then, the station had drifted 2850 kilometres towards Greenland.

- Planes first reached the North Pole in 1948. Since then, expeditions by ship, skidoo, dog sled, submarine and car have all reached the Pole.

- In 1987, Australian Dick Smith became the first person to fly a helicopter there.

- About 30 per cent of the world's untapped oil reserves are located beneath the ice of the Arctic Circle, and a number of countries lay claim to them.

- Each year, about 250 people from around the world run the 42 kilometres of the North Pole Marathon around Barneo Ice Camp.

- The Arctic is warming faster than any other part of the world. Some scientists predict the sea ice will completely disappear during Arctic summer within a generation, and it will then be possible to sail all the way to the North Pole.

4
GOING NORTH

Finally boarding the Antonov An-74 aircraft for the two-hour flight to the floating ice runway at Barneo was a huge relief. At last, we were on our way to the starting point. I was in awe as I looked out the window. In all directions, as far as I could see was white. Peering closely, though, I could see little lines of blue, known as open water leads, and as we got lower, darker lines, which were the shadows from compression ridges buckling the surface.

Barneo is a temporary camp set up each year by the Russian Geographical Society for the summer season. Scientists, pilots, engineers and explorers all use it as their base.

The Russians look for a good area of sea ice, then a team of people jump out of the back of a plane with parachutes.

A couple of tractors and all the tents and gear they will need are dropped onto the ice with them. Their job is then to establish the base and construct the runway. At the end of the season, everything they can't fly out again sinks to the bottom of the ocean as temperatures warm and the sea ice melts.

When we arrived, we headed by helicopter straight to our starting point, which we had decided would be at 88°N 40'. The Russians had told us and all other teams that because of the delays and how thin the sea ice was this year, they had a fixed end date for all expeditions. If we weren't at the Pole by that date, they would be picking us up by helicopter regardless of where we were and taking us back to Barneo. It meant we effectively had only around 12 days to get to the Pole. We did our maths and, after much discussion, decided to make our starting point around 150 kilometres from the Pole, which meant we had to cover greater distances each day than we had originally planned. Importantly, though, we would have air support for evacuation if something went wrong.

At Barneo, I couldn't find anything resembling a female toilet, and there were big Russian military guys carrying guns everywhere, so I figured it was time to try using a pee funnel for the first time, so that I could pee standing up and not worry too much about privacy. I walked over to the area where all the men were standing up to pee in a couple of barrels in the snow, in full sight of everyone, and tried to act confident, like I'd done it a hundred times before. In fact, Dad had been hassling me to practise using the funnel for weeks before we left, and I'd only pretended to listen.

My first attempt failed miserably. My thermal pants under my shell were soaked in my own pee and I tried to downplay it as people walked past me. But I was in tears behind my sunglasses, and I privately decided I wouldn't be using the funnel for the rest of the trip – I was a girl and I was going to pee like one.

Our transport from Barneo to our drop-off was in an Mi-8 helicopter, a huge beast commonly used by the military. It was about 3 am when we took off, but it was approaching summer at the North Pole so the sun was still shining, as it's 24-hour daylight at that time of year.

We shared the Mi-8 with two other teams heading to drop-off points near our own. These would be the longest journeys attempted that season because most other teams had decided to attempt the last degree to the Pole only. I was the only woman on the helicopter and I was surrounded by big men who all had vast expedition experience. One of the teams even had three serious-faced British ex-special forces soldiers. I can only imagine how I must have looked to them: a little 14-year-old girl in her brand-new pink polar shell (sitting in wet pee pants). It was super intimidating.

The Arctic landscape is beyond words and no image online or created in my mind could have prepared me for the real thing.

It was also impossible to prepare for the cold. When we landed it was −29°C and, coming from training on Victorian beaches, it was a completely new kind of cold to me. It seemed insane to think that we had been dropped right in the middle of the frozen Arctic Ocean. There was nothing but white as far as the eye could see and the sun was low in the sky.

By the time we'd stepped out onto the ice, I'd already thought a lot about the challenges we'd face over the coming days. We needed to cover an average of 12.4 kilometres each day to make it to the Pole on time. It doesn't sound like much, but in cold conditions and on rugged terrain, progress is slow. You are almost never skiing in a straight line. The surface is like a maze of cracks and compression zones that have to be negotiated. We all knew this had to be a tightly run expedition.

But the biggest challenge, I thought, would be for sure the mental one. I knew there'd be times when I'd really want to give up, but I remembered what Mum had said, that if I quit I would regret it forever. I wasn't planning on it.

By the time we were dropped off, it had been more than 24 hours since we'd slept. Everyone was tired. Nevertheless, we decided to get moving rather than make camp and rest at the drop-off point. We got off to a good start and it didn't feel as hard as I'd thought it might be. As the day progressed, though, the wind picked up and the going got harder.

We hadn't been skiing long before the rough landscape became more obvious. On the horizon, the ice was cracked and folded. We needed to pick a path that headed north, but it was like an obstacle course. It's difficult enough pulling a

60-kilogram sled across flat ice, when you only weigh about the same, but once we started to encounter ridges of crumbled ice it really became tough. I had to get my ski poles behind me, bury them solidly in the ice and use them to push myself up and over the ridges, hauling the weight of the sled behind me. Pressure ridges are caused by two masses of sea ice colliding with great force, creating rugged ice shards above (and below) the water level. In some cases, they rise about eight metres above the surface. It's not as if they are smooth either – they're bumpy and cracked, sometimes making it hard to find a spot where you can place your skis flat and grip the ice. Sometimes, we had to take off our skis and strap them to the sled while we hauled individual sleds up and over as a team.

It wasn't just exhausting and time-consuming; it was dangerous. The sled hovered at the top of the ridge before tumbling over the edge and down the other side. If you were already on the other side, you had to move quickly as it hurtled down towards you.

It didn't take too long to get used to the conditions, but Dad was struggling with the constant pain from his stent. Not that he told me, of course – the last thing he wanted me to do was worry about him.

To drag our sleds, we attached them to harnesses on our backs that mainly pull from the hips. With every step, the harness was pulling on Dad's stomach and sending a stabbing pain through his groin. Not only that, but his pee was bright red. If that was happening at home, anyone would freak and go straight to the doctor. But I couldn't even guess how far away the nearest doctor was now. If the rough terrain was hard on me, it was even more so on Dad (after arriving home, he confessed it had been like torture).

Surrounding us, though, was a white wonderland. Blocks of blue ice with sheer sides erupted from the landscape, and the ice sometimes formed unusual shapes, like beautiful ice sculptures. While the bigger-picture view was astonishing, we also got down closer to the sea ice to look at some of the crystals. They were like delicate feathers that disintegrated when you touched them.

One of the most bizarre things I discovered in the early part of our journey was the path of the sun. Because we were at the top of Earth, the sun continued to move around us at the same distance above the horizon, never rising, never setting. At home, you can tell roughly where east and west are by tracking the movement of the sun. But it is so different in the Arctic and almost impossible to imagine what it would be like in the Northern Hemisphere winter, when the sun is at the opposite end of the planet and the North Pole is plunged into 24-hour darkness.

Our first day was a success, in my eyes. We only managed to cover 10 kilometres but I'd enjoyed every second of this new lifestyle. By the time we were ready to set up camp, though, I was completely exhausted. I fell asleep on my sleeping mat in its chair position inside the tent, fully clothed in my polar shell, while Dad made our first dehydrated dinner.

❄

One of my favourite things about life on the ice is the silence. I will never be able to properly explain this, but when there is an absence of wind, the only sound is the noise that you make. The ever-changing ocean currents cause the ice to shift, so occasionally the stillness is broken by what is almost a symphony of groaning and wailing made by the movement of the ice. It was a constant reminder that we were skiing on frozen water and, if we ever misjudged our path, we could possibly plunge through the ice into the freezing ocean below. On average the ice is no more than two metres thick. In some places, it was incredibly thin and we were careful to avoid the darker-looking ice that indicated water was not far beneath us.

We came to a few spots where an open water lead exposed the ocean. Falling into that water would have certainly been the end of the trip, but it was also extremely cool to get this perspective. It looked a bit like a river, with thick crusts of ice forming the banks. There are a few options when you come across a lead. One is to change course and follow it to see if it closes up again, but that might have taken us kilometres off course and we were already on a tight schedule. Another was to make a small floating bridge from the sleds and carefully move across to the other side. The final option is a bit more extreme – and to keep us on course, at one point Eric decided that this was what we would do. First, he would swim across, then pull Dad, Petter and myself across by rope on a raft made from our sleds. He put on a dry suit (otherwise known as an immersion suit), which is both buoyant and waterproof, and slid carefully into the water. He had to be sure to keep his face out of the icy water, as the suit's opening for his face was the only place water could get in. He managed the manoeuvre successfully and stroked across the 10 or so metres of ocean, pulling his sled behind him. There was a little ledge of ice on the other side of the lead and Eric pulled himself and the sled out of the water. Dad and I roped our sleds together and I carefully climbed aboard, one knee and one hand on either sled, then Eric slowly pulled me across the open ocean. Dad yelled jokingly across to us just before he climbed onto the sleds: 'If I get this wrong, Jade, your North Pole dream could be over.' He was just stirring though and, thankfully, the crossing went without any mishaps.

No matter how hard you train, nothing can prepare you for the tedious hours of the constant movement of skiing across the ice all day – my neck and shoulders became incredibly sore.

Surprisingly, the low temperatures didn't feel too bad as long as we were moving, but it always felt painfully cold when we stopped at breaks, especially lunch. The bitter chill would seep in and the moisture from my breath would freeze my face mask to my skin. Once we started skiing again it would take a while for my body to reheat. However, some parts – my fingers mainly – would stay cold and ache with a pain so intense that I still cannot really describe it, especially after going to the toilet during the breaks. We were not far into the journey when I realised that toileting would be one of the worst aspects of the trip for me. Compared to the guys, it took me a lot longer. I had multiple zips and layers of clothes to manage, which meant I had to take my big polar mitts off and be in just liner mitts. I decided I had to walk away from the group and find a stack of ice to hide behind. I'm sure Dad and the others thought I was being a bit precious, but I wanted to maintain at least a little bit of dignity. It was already in short supply after walking away from the group carrying a roll of toilet paper. The average temperature during our trip was −27°C and it soon became obvious there was absolutely nothing comfortable about a comfort stop. Once I'd dropped my pants for a pee the tops of my legs and my butt were exposed to the brutal conditions.

❄

On one of our first mornings, Eric called Victor, our liaison person at Barneo, to confirm our position, and received some daunting news. The ice runway had cracked again. They needed to attempt to build another one to get us out. They'd also cancelled all the incoming flights from Longyearbyen, which meant the North Pole Marathon had been cancelled, along with Dixie's expedition and another family's.

The uncertainty of the situation put me on edge. Without an operating runway, there was no real way we could get off the sea ice and back home. I'm not a morning person at the best of times, but this worry made me extra snappy. Luckily, Dad was aware of this and was incredibly patient when I wasn't in the best of moods. It's not easy sharing a tent with anyone, let alone your dad, and there must have been moments when he wanted to let off some steam, too. Luckily for me, he held back!

It was thanks to Dad that I was able to attempt such a trip in the first place. I couldn't have done it without him. But as the days went by I could see that he was in serious pain. The plastic stent between his bladder and kidney was supposed to be removed a few days after the surgery, but because we'd flown out the same day, it had to stay inside him for over a month. He kept joking that every time he peed and left a bright red bloodstain on the white landscape, he was leaving a trail for the polar bears to find us. Not entirely funny, since polar bears can smell blood from up to 20 kilometres away.

We did have plenty of laughs, despite the harsh conditions – or perhaps because of them. Lunch quickly became one of the highlights of the day, even if it involved eating frozen salami, which is almost impossible to bite into. As we were sitting on our sleds one day digging into dry biscuits, Dad asked me what I'd be eating if I was at home. I knew straight away: avocado smash and goat's cheese on sourdough toast with tomato and salt and pepper. Everyone else groaned and called me cruel for teasing them.

When you're travelling across floating sea ice, you are at the mercy of the ocean currents. If the ocean movement was away from the Pole – known as negative drift – we could literally be going nowhere each day and really struggle to reach the

Pole in time. However, we had a strong easterly drift for most of the trip and, on one night, even drifted two kilometres closer to the Pole. I was pretty chuffed about that.

Eric wanted to help me learn as much as I could about the polar environment during our first time on the ice together, so one day he taught me how to navigate using the sun, and encouraged me to take the lead. Most of the time, the four of us travelled in single file in the tracks Eric laid first. Soon I found I really enjoyed being out the front – knowing that you're the first person to have walked there is an incredible feeling.

But the isolation can also be intimidating. We were reminded of some of the dangers out there when Eric spotted polar bear tracks in the snow. They were very clear and so big I could fit my entire hand in one. Eric had done this trip many times before and he told me he was constantly looking around us and even over his shoulder in case of a bear in sight. This was a huge bear, he said, and its tracks were quite fresh. I started looking over my shoulder too.

In recent years, with the changing climate, polar bears have had to travel further over the ice to find what little prey is left in that part of the world. They don't really seek people out, but if they haven't eaten in a long time, or feel threatened, they will attack and kill. The sad truth is, we are a much bigger threat to polar bears than they are to us. They spend 50 per cent of their time hunting, mostly for seals, but the loss of ice is affecting them greatly. As they become less likely to find food in the wild, they spend longer on shore and often come into contact with communities, resulting in interactions that usually end badly for the bears. Scientists estimate the wild population of polar bears to be somewhere between 22,000 and 31,000. These numbers are already in decline, and the US listed the species as threatened in 2008. I fear for these beautiful creatures and for this entire environment if something isn't done about the changing climate soon.

During the day, as we were skiing, there was a lot of time to think, and I thought a lot about the fact that this part of the world might not be accessible in just a few years' time due to global warming. There was even a possibility we could be the last people ever to reach the North Pole; all those cracks in the runway may have been a sign. So I decided it was important for me to capture as many memories and as much footage of this amazing environment as I could. Soon I would be back at home in my everyday routine, but for the moment it was anything but everyday. Being constantly aware of where I was and being grateful for the opportunity became my goal for the rest of the trip.

On day six, we hit the halfway mark. We'd pushed so hard already to get to this point, but we still had another 75 kilometres to go. Eric was very encouraging, telling me he admired my stamina and determination. Out there, every little bit of support helped.

We'd been away from home for almost three weeks now, and I was getting pretty homesick. Fortunately, I was able to call home on the satellite phone every day, even if it was only for a couple of minutes. It immediately made me feel better, even though Mum and I spent most of our time talking about Dad and how he was coping with the pain.

By the time we got to the eighth day of the trip, we were ready for our final push towards the North Pole, but in the morning before we'd packed up the camp we got a radio call from Victor back at the base. The landing strip at Barneo still wasn't fixed, and the ground conditions for the rest of the trip were forecast to be very tough with extensive compression zones. Plus, we only had five days to reach the Pole before the season ended, and they would pick us up regardless of whether we'd reached the Pole or not.

Overnight the wind had picked right up, and when we went outside in the morning our tents and sleds had been completely covered by snow. Up to that point it had been all sunshine and blue skies, but suddenly it was overcast and the visibility was really low. At least the wind was blowing towards the Pole, as a headwind could have pushed us backwards.

The landscape was beautiful – like a frozen white ocean – but the wind made it even colder than we'd become used to and the terrain became more rugged and slowed us down as we dragged our sleds over the increasing number of compression zones. The horizon was chaos, with no clear route to follow.

Dad was still struggling with the pain and for the first time it was really affecting his pace. The harness pushing up against the plastic stent caused him sharp pain and the ups and downs of the terrain exacerbated the movement. Eric admitted to us after the trip that at one stage he had seriously considered having Dad evacuated – it was his job to make sure we arrived at our destination safely, after all – but I'm glad it never got to that point. I think Dad was more worried about being the reason we didn't make it than he was about his own health.

The worst part was that the terrain continued to deteriorate. Even Eric was struggling, and at times it took three of us, as Petter was filming, to get each other's sleds over the ice rubble. It was almost as if the landscape was fighting us from every angle. Surprisingly, we still managed to cover 14.5 kilometres most days, which just shows how far a little persistence could take us.

When Eric mentioned on day 10 that we were the most northerly people in the world at that point in time, it blew my mind. I imagined us on the top of a little toy globe. As we settled down for the night it really sank in that, unless something went horribly wrong, we were going to reach the Pole the next day.

On what was supposed to be our final day, I woke feeling incredibly excited. Eric had heard from Victor that the Barneo runway was operable again, so once we got to the Pole it seemed highly likely that we'd be able to get out. The conditions had eased and now there was just a light wind.

At our last drink break before the Pole, we looked up to see an Air Berlin plane fly over our heads. I think it was filled with tourists doing a sightseeing North Pole flyover. Obviously, that's a pleasant and far easier way to see this magnificent landscape, but there was no way I would have swapped my experience on foot for any number of scenic flights.

Eric gave me the GPS and told me to take the lead and find 90°N. It was strange to see the GPS just click over to nine-zero and almost unbelievable that we had finally made it. I turned to Eric in disbelief and he assured me that we were there. It was just our luck that at the time we arrived at the Pole, it was in the middle of a large compression zone, which meant dragging our sleds the last few minutes to our final objective was super hard work. There is no permanent marker at the North Pole because the sea ice is very quickly drifting on the ocean currents.

It was snowing lightly and Dad and Eric both gave me a big hug, which isn't easy when you're wearing skis and attached to a sled.

I was now the youngest person ever to have skied to the North Pole from anywhere outside the last degree, and it was one of the greatest feelings in the world. All the hard work had paid off. We celebrated by sticking a ski pole into the snow where the North Pole would be, and I ran around the world, crossing every line of longitude in a matter of seconds – again, my mind was blown.

Dad went over to his sled and pulled out a little parcel – a present from my brother, Kane. He had made me a painting with the words: 'Limits are illusions that we create to protect ourselves from ourselves.' It captured the moment perfectly.

Dad also handed me a letter from Mum.

To my dearest baby girl, Jade. If you are reading this letter it's because you have just reached your goal of the North Pole.

Wow! Wow! Wow! Breathe deeply and enjoy every second of what you have just achieved. I feel like I have been with you every step. I could not be any prouder of you than I am, having watched you grow from a small baby to a beautiful, happy, courageous, strong young woman. You amaze me every day.
I love you so much and I love you more. Mum xx

Our final day also happened to coincide with Anzac Day, the day Australians and New Zealanders remember the sacrifices made by our armed service men and women. I hadn't missed the annual Dawn Service at the Shrine of Remembrance since I was born, so we decided to hold our own small service on the ice. Dad read the story of the youngest Anzac – a 14-year-old boy. Then he played the Last Post on his iPhone and together, we sang the national anthem.

I placed a note I had written in a sealed container and buried it in the ice. I knew the ice would drift towards warmer oceans and eventually melt and then my note would wash up on a beach somewhere, hopefully to be opened and read by someone in the future.

Finally, we set up camp, excited to be sleeping at the Pole, even though we were already drifting away from it on ocean currents.

We'd only just settled in and I'd just called home when the call came through that the Russians were on their way to get us, so we had to pack up all our gear again. I was on a toilet break when I heard the helicopter approaching and had to run back to the others while doing up my pants. Eric went out into the snow to direct the helicopter towards us and, as it dropped out of the sky, he disappeared in a flurry of white. It was quite spectacular. We hauled our sleds and ourselves onto the helicopter and took off for Barneo, leaving the Pole behind.

CLIMATE CHANGE IN EARTH'S POLAR REGIONS

In 1988, the World Meteorological Organization and the United Nations Environment Program established the Intergovernmental Panel on Climate Change (IPCC). Drawing on the work of more than 800 experts, in 2013 the IPCC released a 2000-page report that found the atmosphere and ocean systems are warming, and that it is extremely likely that human influence is the dominant cause.

The emission of greenhouse gases, such as carbon dioxide, methane and nitrous oxide (all of which are produced during the burning of fossil fuels or the production of oil, coal and natural gas), contributes to this warming of our atmosphere. While this has always occurred to some extent in what is known as the carbon cycle, the natural carbon cycle has been distorted by the introduction of excess greenhouse gases. For 400,000 years, carbon levels in the atmosphere never surpassed 300 parts per million. In 2013, CO_2 levels exceeded 400 parts per million for the first time ever.

Some of the most damaging effects of climate change can be seen in Earth's polar regions. Seventy per cent of Earth's fresh water is frozen, and the summer ice melts in both the Arctic and Antarctic have become increasingly severe. Not only does this raise sea levels and cause coastal flooding, it also completely adjusts the world's major ocean currents.

In addition, the higher levels of CO_2 in the atmosphere are also being absorbed by oceans and making them acidic, which is incredibly harmful for marine life.

Climate change is a real and serious threat we all need to be aware of and work together to act on. Despite peoples' various countries, religions, beliefs and genders, we are one people and we all need to work together if we are to make positive change for the future generations of the planet. It's not about saving the planet – Earth will be here and recover long after we have gone – it's about saving the human species.

5
PART ONE COMPLETE

Coming home was a really strange and challenging transition for me. I'd travelled across the frozen Arctic Ocean. I'd reached the North Pole. I felt like I had changed, grown as a person and experienced so much, but at home not much had changed. It was a weird feeling – both comforting and disconcerting.

Thanks to a couple of days in a hotel in Longyearbyen before our flight home, I'd already had all the things I'd craved while I was out on the ice – a hot shower and some great food. But seeing Mum and Kane was the best. I'd missed them so much.

The school year was obviously well underway but, thankfully, I still had a few days to adjust before I had to go back. And there was a lot of adjusting to do. The media off the back

59

of the trip started the day after we arrived back in Melbourne. I'd never had any media training (nor have I to this day), so I was miles out of my comfort zone (again!). The newspaper and magazine interviews weren't too bad, but radio and TV were harder because it was live to air and there was nowhere to hide from tough questions. Everyone was super nice to me though, and I am very grateful to the media community for being so supportive of what I was trying to achieve. It was full-on, but a great opportunity to share my experiences with others. As the days back home ticked over, deep down all I really wanted was to be back in the Arctic. I missed the silence and the connection I had with my self and my mind. Back home, especially with the media, I had no opportunity to debrief and process what I'd just experienced – there was always a distraction.

Dad had also checked back into hospital. The plastic stent between his kidney and bladder was finally being taken out. The surgeon said it had become very calcified and had been shredding away at his insides while he was dragging his sled. Thinking back on it, I honestly don't know how he managed to push through. He is the strongest person I know. My post-trip physical issues seemed mild by comparison. I had some frost nip, which is the first stage of frostbite, on my thighs and bum from going to the toilet. The feeling in the ends of my fingers hadn't yet returned; it was going to be a little while before all the blisters on my feet healed; and I was looking and feeling rather scrawny and weak. Despite eating about three times as many calories as normal while on the expedition, I'd lost a fair bit of weight. Aside from the work of dragging the sled and skiing, our bodies had had to work really hard to create heat and stay warm.

My friends organised a surprise dinner for me. After not seeing them for almost a month, it was so good to catch up. We didn't really pick over all the details of the trip. There were a few questions and then we just got back to our usual gossip and laughter.

We didn't really speak much about it at home, either, after the initial excitement of our return. These expeditions were not unusual in our house and were never a feature of conversation for more than a few days. We just picked up with our usual family routine.

I knew the experience had changed me, though, in ways I couldn't really grasp yet at fourteen. I knew for sure that I wanted more adventure and I was conscious that, in another 12 months, we'd be heading north again, this time to Greenland.

This next expedition was going to be almost four times as far, meaning I had to be even more prepared. So, after a month's break, it was back to the gym. Unfortunately, the break had been long enough for me to lose all the strength I'd built up in the year I'd spent training for the North Pole. My first session back was incredibly frustrating. We'd done a cross-country run at school the day before, so my legs were already tired, but I still thought I'd be able to smash out 10 rounds of 10 back squats like usual. Wrong! I only got to the sixth round before my legs started cramping up and I had to stop. I spent the rest of the session on the foam roller in tears, trying to ease some of the tightness. Much to my horror, I was going to have to start from scratch.

In the months that followed, I spent my time getting back into school, gradually increasing my training and being involved in the occasional media commitment. I also celebrated my fifteenth birthday!

I continued to be thrown outside my comfort zone and challenged by a few major new experiences that accelerated my journey of personal growth. The first was an invitation to deliver a TEDx talk in Melbourne. TED talks are based around 'ideas worth spreading' and are designed to inspire conversations and connections. When Dad asked me if it was something I wanted to do I knew my answer straight away and replied 'Yes!' He later told me that if they'd asked him, he would have needed a week to think about it and even then he may have said no out of fear.

I'd seen a few TED talks online before and loved them, but I really had no idea what I was in for. For starters, I wasn't sure what I would want to talk about and I'd never really even spoken in public, other than at school assemblies – certainly not to a massive live audience and multiple cameras. But, just like skiing, I decided I wasn't going to let my lack of experience stop me and I'd give it my best shot. This was going to be a very new and different kind of adventure.

TEDx offers all its speakers training in constructing their talks and learning to present them effectively. Jon Yeo, the convenor of TEDx Melbourne, organised weekly sessions with me where he taught me the 'TED style' of presenting and we brainstormed the big idea I wanted to share. I decided to focus my talk on shifting the focus of young women from how we appear, to the possibilities of what we can do. My journey to the North Pole really confirmed this message for me – polar expeditions are far from glamorous and I needed to focus all my energy into becoming physically strong in order to make it happen, rather than seeking to meet body-stereotypes portrayed on social media. I set about writing my speech and practising how I would present it.

The other exciting milestone on the horizon was the release of the 40-minute Nat Geo documentary Petter shot on our way to the North Pole. It was due to be released in August, but I was able to watch a rough cut at the offices of WTFN one night after school. I absolutely loved it, and it brought back some of the unreal memories we'd shared on the trip. *On Thin Ice: Jade's Polar Dream* would be released later in the year. As part of the lead-up to the film's release, I was invited to the National Geographic headquarters in Washington DC to attend their annual Explorers Symposium 2016. The National Geographic Society supports a number of people working in field-based science and conservation, and each year they bring all of them together for a few days to share their discoveries. Surprisingly, my brother and I were the only young people there and I was so inspired by the speakers on stage. My mind continued to expand with possibilities.

The whole time we were away in the USA, my forthcoming TEDx talk had been on my mind and I used whatever spare time I had to work on it. I practised a lot – maybe an hour every day for the two months in the lead-up. My talk only went for about 10 minutes, but I committed to hundreds of hours of preparation and practice beforehand. By the time the event arrived, I had become crazy bored with it.

Dad helped me prepare by acting as my test audience and critic. He told me that if I started feeling really anxious and nervous before my talk, I shouldn't try to calm myself down. By far the easiest way to manage nerves is to shift those feelings to a mindset of excitement. The feelings of nervousness and excitement are closely linked, so it's an easier switch to make than trying to calm down. Dad told me to just breathe deeply and smile – it worked.

There were 1300 people in the audience on the day. Most of my family and close friends were in the front row. I didn't look in that direction, knowing that one of my friends might crack me up, but the stage lights were very bright so I couldn't really make out any faces anyway. Occasionally the crowd would break into spontaneous applause after I said something and I just responded with multiple thank yous – a result of the nerves. But the talk was over before I knew it and it was so practised that the words just flowed out of my mouth.

I gave a few other smaller talks, but one of the other big ones I gave that year was at ImagiNATION (previously named National Young Leaders Day), organised by a group called Halogen who runs events for young Australian school leaders. Events were held in Sydney, Melbourne and Brisbane for grade five and six student leaders from across each state, and I spoke to a combined audience of more than 12,000 kids and their teachers. Having these young people respond so positively to my own message of choosing bravery over perfection was incredibly rewarding.

After ImagiNATION, I had to say no to virtually all speaking requests so I could focus on my schoolwork and being a teenager. Becoming a professional public speaker isn't one of my ambitions, but if an opportunity comes up to make a big impact with an audience I care about, I'll try to make it happen.

Next, I packed my bags for another three weeks in the USA. The first part of the trip was with my school as part of a program touring the Ivy League colleges on the east coast. It really opened me up to the possibilities of education abroad in the future, and New York City is definitely now one of my favourite places in the world.

After the college tour, I said goodbye to my school friends at Los Angeles airport and, while they returned home, I met up with my aunt, who was living there at the time, and spent a couple of nights with her. As always, it was so much fun. I attended a preview screening of my North Pole movie, *On Thin Ice*, at SoHo House in West Hollywood. Again, it brought so many memories flooding back and got me super hyped for the trip to Greenland the following year. Plus, I also met some very inspiring people. Some of the members of the DiCaprio Foundation attended the screening – not Leo himself, unfortunately, but his mum, Irmelin Indenbirken and her partner, David Ward, were in the audience. The Foundation does lots of powerful work in conservation and I'm hoping I will have the opportunity to collaborate with them in the future.

When I got back to Australia, just before *On Thin Ice* was shown on National Geographic channels around the world, I was incredibly honoured to be named Young Adventurer of the Year 2016 by the Australian Geographic Society. On the night in Sydney, David Suzuki flew in from Canada to be the guest speaker. He is an incredible human who has dedicated his life to saving our planet from climate change. He gave an inspiring speech about recognising that all humans are one and we need to work together to make a difference. Honestly, I think I was more excited to speak to him later in the evening than when receiving the award itself.

It topped off an amazing year. But now, I had to focus my mind on the upcoming Greenland crossing and mentally prepare myself for what was going to be a much longer and tougher journey than the one to the North Pole. It was also going to be a really good test for the Antarctic trip we were planning to undertake six months after that. I was apprehensive and a lot of it would be new to me but still, I was ready to commit to the process and enjoy the second chapter of the journey.

THAT TEDx TALK

What if young women around the world were encouraged to be more rather than less? What if the focus shifted from how we appear to the possibilities of what we can do? As a young woman, I live in a world where I am constantly bombarded with messages to be less. To eat less. To wear less. To be skinnier. To shrink my ambitions to fit in. To wait for my Prince Charming to come and save me. Or to avoid activities that are 'for boys' because I'm not strong enough or as tough. These messages fuel my fears and insecurities and I'm then left wondering, all the time, whether I'm good enough or whether I should just play it safe so I don't end up making myself look silly. But imagine if all the young women in a particular country took one step forward in terms of the level of belief of their own possibilities. How much brighter would the future of that country be? Now imagine if all the young women on this planet took that same step forward in their thinking as to what is possible for themselves. How much brighter would the future of our world be? Now that's adventurous thinking. And, by the way, it's so much more fun to try to be more rather than less.

In April this year, at the age of 14, I became the youngest person in history, male or female, to ski to the North Pole from anywhere outside the last degree. It was also the longest journey to the Pole by any woman on the planet for the past two years. I dragged a sled that was as heavy as me over a distance of 150 kilometres as measured from the Pole on skis in −30°C temperatures. One hundred and fifty kilometres might not sound too bad until you understand the environment up there on the Arctic Ocean. We had to ski our way around or over compression zones where sea ice had collided to make ice rubble. Sometimes the ice rubble can become walls of ice metres high. We also had to find our way around open water leads where the sea ice had split. We would build a bridge out of our sleds or someone would have to swim across in an immersion suit while the rest of us were dragged across on a raft made from our sleds. We were travelling on sea ice so the ocean currents were constantly dragging us off course and we would often hear the ice crack beneath us and wonder whether we'd fall through into the freezing ocean below. We also crossed polar bear tracks and would stay awake in our tents listening for them. Not that we could sleep anyway, since there's 24-hour daylight up there at this time of year. I'm not a skier either. I only learned to ski a year before on a three-day trip to New Zealand. There's not much snow where I live, so I trained every day for virtually a year beforehand, including dragging tyres behind me, which is pretty close to the real thing. As you can imagine, the going was slow and hard. Apart from a few blisters, I lost the feeling in the tips of my fingers, which eventually came back after all the skin had died and peeled back. The worst part of all was I got frost nip on my upper thighs and bum from having to expose myself to the freezing cold and wind every time I went to the toilet. But I loved it. It was the best experience of my life so far, and I fell in love with this beautiful but fragile part of the planet. As much as I couldn't wait to get home to see family and friends, I was sad to leave.

Next April, my plan is to ski 540 kilometres across Greenland, aged fifteen. Then, at the end of next year, ski 1170 kilometres from the coast of Antarctica to the South Pole [at this stage we were planning to ski the traditional route]. By then I'll be sixteen. If I can get there, apart from a few minor records, I'll be the youngest person to ski to both Poles and to complete the Polar Hat-Trick.

So what have I learned in my brief life so far that might be worth sharing? I have learned that all those messages I receive daily to be less are wrong. I have learned that by expanding my dreams it has been impossible to think about shrinking. Instead of focusing on how we look, let's focus on what our bodies and minds can do and discover the incredible possibilities that we are capable of and can contribute to this world. There is nothing wrong with trying to improve your physique. The problem is when people sacrifice their capability or their health for the sake of fitting in to some visual standard shaped by other people. Let's make it about what you do rather than how you look. The funny thing about many popular social media fitness accounts is that they post pictures of themselves standing in front of a mirror doing nothing. That's not inspiring. That's just trying to make the rest of us feel bad. I think it's much more inspiring to see photos and videos of people actually doing something.

So how do we change things? How do we shift our focus? For me, when I see other women go forward without fear I learn what is possible. There are some amazing examples of young women in history choosing to be more. But just as amazing to me are the girls who work part-time while studying to support their families. Girls who stand up for what they believe in. Girls who get up before dawn to train for the sport they love. Girls who stay up late studying hard to make the most of their education. Any girl who refuses to buy into the messaging to be less. If you are my parent, my relative, my teacher or my coach then I'm talking to you. Don't be overprotective of me just because I am a girl. Encourage me to take risks in chasing dreams that are important to me, not you.

The sisterhood. Let's celebrate the achievements of our girlfriends. Don't cut them down. I've been amazed at the support I have received from my friends. But most important of all, we must start with ourselves. We are our own worst enemies. We need to get out of our own way and stop caring so much about what other people think. The truth is everybody else is worried about what everybody else thinks about them. We need to focus on what we want for ourselves in line with our own personal values, not those of our parents or our friends or the school we attend. Don't do it for others; do it for you. To expand what we believe is possible we must have courage. We must be prepared and willing to fail. Don't wait until you think you can do something perfectly, just get started. I had only really been skiing once in my life before and then I tried to ski to the North Pole, which is pretty funny when I stop and think about it. I also tried peeing standing up with a pee funnel in −20°C temperatures and I failed terribly. I spent the rest of the day skiing in pants that were covered in my own frozen pee. Courage is not the absence of fear but the willingness to take action despite the presence of fear or self-doubt. Without bravery our lives remain small. So let's all commit to take one step forward in our thinking and in our expectations as to what is possible for young women to achieve. Let's constantly check ourselves that we are focusing on what we can do, not how we appear. All those small steps will soon add up and we will collectively expand what is possible for young women and, as a result, for the future of our world.

Funny photo of me wearing a pink hoodie with a fur ruff when I was only four
years old!

My brother and me at Everest Base Camp in 2013. I was 12 and Kane was 10.

Me at 13 years old when I started trying to put muscle on for my polar journeys.

Where I live, the only way to really train for pulling a sled is to drag a tyre on the beach.

Dad and me training in Svalbard before heading off on our North Pole expedition.

Dad hauling his sled through the ice rubble during the North Pole expedition.

Pressure ridges can run for miles, so often there is no choice but to climb them and haul your sled over.

On the frozen Arctic Ocean, currents and ice movement pull the ice apart and create open sections of water called 'leads'.

Skiing on thin ice on our way to the North Pole.

GREENLAND CROSSING

EXPEDITION 2

Destination: Greenland, crossing of second largest ice cap in the world

Distance: 550 kilometres

Duration: 27 days, May–June 2017

Goal: Youngest woman in history to complete the crossing

Team: Me, Dad, guide Eric Philips, camerawoman Frederique Olivier, camera assistant Heath Jamieson

Big challenges: Getting to the start, unusually warm weather, sunstroke, dehydration, katabatic winds, wet blizzards, polar bears

Everyday challenges: No shower, minimal changes of clothes, dehydrated food, hunger, early-morning wake-ups and zero privacy

6
GREENLAND'S WARM WELCOME

After departing Melbourne, those familiar feelings had already set in by the time we had landed in transit in Dubai – while we were out on the ice, what would I be missing back home? My brother and Mum were the ones I'd missed most when we were in the North Pole, and I knew it would be the same over the coming weeks in Greenland.

I was also going to miss my friends; staying in touch with what everyone was doing through social media was a big part of my everyday life. My North Pole expedition was the first time I had truly disconnected from the constant stimulation of the online world. It took a while to let go of that world and instead focus on the present, on the basic necessities of survival and on the beauty of my surroundings.

We landed in Denmark after 29 hours of travel from Melbourne and very little sleep. Almost immediately, I was embracing the change of scenery and the thrill of experiencing new things.

After a quick shower and a change of clothes, we met up with our camerawoman for this expedition, Frederique Olivier. We then headed straight to the Danish Meteorological Institute in Copenhagen to interview John Cappelen, the senior climatologist at DMI, for the new Nat Geo documentary – National Geographic jumped on board again for the final two chapters of my polar journey, producing a feature-length documentary due for release in 2018. John is responsible for recording and forecasting the weather in Greenland, which is part of the Danish realm.

He told us there were many DMI weather stations located across Greenland. The stations send back data at least once an hour to be collected and analysed by John's team. The oldest data series dates back to 1784.

'I can see it in my data every day,' John told me. 'There's no doubt in my mind that global warming is a reality. No doubt at all. It's a fact temperatures are rising in Greenland and they have been on the rise sharply in the last two decades.' He also confirmed he believes the Arctic is warming faster than other parts of the planet – something I was about to find out for myself.

The next day we flew out of Copenhagen and into Kanger-lussuaq on the West coast of Greenland, our final destination before we began. Here we met up with the final two members of our team: Eric Philips – our guide from the North Pole – and Heath Jamieson, who was Frederique's assistant, and would be hauling all the extra weight of the camera equipment and a lot of Frederique's personal gear in his sled so that she could be more mobile.

There is sooooo much that goes on behind the scenes to even get to the starting point of these expeditions, including several tasks that had to be completed a few days before flying out to ensure everything is packed and ready to go. One of the biggest jobs is preparing the food bags, which are stuffed with calorie-dense meals and snacks. We all spent a whole day slicing and bagging salami and cheese, removing wrappers from muesli bars and chocolate (any unnecessary wrapping had to be dumped before we started or we'd just end up carrying excess weight in our sleds), and neatly packing everything into separate day bags – each one identical in its contents.

There were plenty of other last-minute adjustments and preparations to be made. We even needed to sew tiny neoprene nose guards to our ski goggles to give us extra protection from the sun. We also got some rope out and Eric reminded me how to tie a prusik knot (the type of friction hitch I'd been taught by Dean in New Zealand two years earlier) and use it to pull myself out of a crevasse.

We decided to hook ropes and harnesses onto a high fence surrounding the airport and were using them to haul ourselves up when a big angry Greenlandic man came hurtling towards us in his car and very agressively told us to get off the fence and find somewhere else to practise our skills. Apparently, airport security wasn't too happy with a trio of Aussies appearing to climb the security fence. We really hadn't thought that one through.

Our last task was to pack our sleds in the most efficient way possible, like not packing anything sharp near an air mattress (unless, of course, you want to sleep on the cold ice and snow). Much of the load seemed to be food and fuel (which we took in cardboard boxes) – heavy items like these, we put in the middle of the sled. Apart from that, we had packed a lot of the same gear as we had for the North Pole trip, like tents, our sleeping bags, and a stove and pot for melting snow. Clothing is kept to an absolute minimum – mostly just one of everything, but allowing for a few changes of socks and underwear. Eric confessed he had only packed two pairs of underwear. I, on the other hand, believed it was perfectly normal to pack 15 pairs.

We'd been in Kangerlussuaq for a few days, and John's words about global warming were already proving undeniable. While prepping during the day, we spent a lot of our time working outside and had all been dressed only in track pants and t-shirts. It was so warm. I had expected the cold on the coast of Greenland to be biting already, but it wasn't close.

The day we were due to start our 550-kilometre crossing, the sky was dark and, instead of snow, it was pouring rain, so we were forced to extend our stay on the coast until the weather cleared up enough for us to begin. We unpacked some of our gear and settled in for another night of comfort and warmth in a real bed.

The next morning the rain had mostly cleared and we were good to go. We got a lift with two other Danish teams, on a huge bus with special wheels designed for the rock and snow, to our start point at the edge of the glacier. I sat up the front next to the driver and he told me I was the youngest person he'd ever driven up to the glacier and he was going to write about me on his Facebook page.

Usually there would have been ice all the way to the drop-off point, but large portions had melted and exposed the dirt and rock below for a long way in the direction we were to start hauling sleds. The sleds aren't particularly delicate, but there was no way we could strap them to our harnesses and drag them across the rough ground. It was all hands on deck so, one by one, four people per heavy, fully-loaded sled, we carried them up over steep, slippery surfaces and through slushy, muddy puddles of dirt and melting snow, with frequent rest stops, until we reached the edge of the retreating glacier a couple of kilometres from where we'd been dropped. Then we'd go back and get the next one and start the process all over again – five sleds in total, between 70 and 110 kilograms each. It was hot, sweaty work and quite unlike anything I'd expected to encounter on the second largest ice cap on the planet.

I wore a mitten on the hand that was gripping the rope at my corner of the sled, not because it was cold, but to stop the weight of the sled tearing the skin on my hand. We had to keep changing positions on each sled to give our hands and arms a rest. My clothes were soaked with sweat by the time we'd finished and the only footwear we had with us were big polar boots rated to −100°C, so our feet were cooking and I had my first few blisters already.

If I needed any proof that Greenland was going to be a completely different experience from the North Pole, now was it. We had finally reached the edge of the ice, but the struggle over the rocks to get to the starting line of the ice cap had already put us well behind our daily goal. We were only carrying 30 days' worth of food and fuel and we had just used up one of them.

Added to that, I was already feeling frustrated at the prospect of needing to re-establish new daily routines again. These expeditions are all about creating habits and having everything in a good place for easy access. The first few days of these trips for me were always the toughest and a struggle to recreate order out of chaos.

Once we were finally on the glacier and rigged up to our sleds, Eric delivered his pre-trip pep talk. We'd skied to the North Pole together, so he had already seen me in action, but I was inspired by his faith in me. It gave me confidence as I took my first steps on the ice towards the other coast.

SOME COOL FACTS ABOUT ...

Greenland

- Greenland is a massive island – it's almost as big as Western Australia – that sits between the North Atlantic and Arctic oceans.

- In fact, it's the biggest island in the world (Australia is a continental landmass).

- There's not a lot of green in Greenland – about 80 per cent of the landmass is covered in snow and ice.

- It's believed Erik the Red, a Viking who was exiled from Iceland, settled here and called it Greenland in the hope the name would attract more settlers.

- Only about 56,000 people live in Greenland (17,000 in the capital, Nuuk), making it the least densely populated territory in the world. As a comparison, about the same number of people live in Wagga Wagga.

- Most of the people who live there are Kalaallit (Inuit for the indigenous people of Greenland).

- Greenland is an autonomous Danish territory, which means the country has its own democratically elected parliament.

- There are no roads anywhere on the island. Instead everyone gets around by plane, boat, helicopter, snowmobile or dog sled.

7

A SLOW START

The terrain up the ice fall from the West coast of Greenland was as unbelievably challenging as it was beautiful. As far as the eye could see, there were rolling hills and valleys of ice.

At this point, we hadn't even strapped on our skis. Instead, we had spent most of our time walking in crampons (metal spikes that attach to boots to grip the slippery ice), and it was not easy. To get up the hills, it was a slow grind of wedging the ski poles in the ice behind me, leaning my weight forward and into the poles, then using them to push myself upwards and make some ground, then repeating the same process until reaching the top. Once at the peak, I had to pull the sled over the edge then run fast enough to the bottom of the hill to outrun it and dodge its plunge, but not so fast that I ended up falling over. Surprisingly, I managed to coordinate and get it right the first time.

Sometimes we even had to work as a team to move individual sleds over steep sections. On these occasions, I was harnessed to my sled with Dad and Eric pushing and tugging at it to get it over the bigger hills at the same time as I was pulling it.

We used up an enormous amount of energy getting each of the five sleds up and over the terrain, sometimes one at a time, and the progress was often so slow I felt as if we were getting nowhere. Along the way, it grew so warm I was wearing only my thin thermal top and a cap to shield my face from the sun.

In between the rolling hills of the ice fall were the ice melts – big ponds of incredibly blue water – and we had to divert to track a course around them. It was like navigating a maze. Eric often decided to take less direct routes, searching for gentler slopes so that we could pull our own sleds over them without needing help from the rest of the team. Often he would ditch his sled and ski off to check a particular route, only to return and advise we had to backtrack to see if we could find a better way forward. Because we weren't travelling in a straight line, we were covering a lot more distance than the 550 kilometres of the crossing as measured in a straight line on a map. This messed with my head and frustrated me.

It was really hard to get used to walking in my crampons, and it took me much longer to get my footing right than Eric and Dad, who had used crampons many times before. It was already a lot different from skiing across the frozen Arctic Ocean.

On multiple occasions, my sled would tip over the top of a ridge and drag me down the slope with it. Sometimes, the sled ended up in a pool of water, but fortunately it floated on the surface – I would imagine myself getting pulled down by my sled and into the icy water.

It went on like this for days. Although we'd managed to find a reasonably flat spot to set up camp on our first night, the next day it was more of the same, like a game of snakes and ladders. It was a huge mental challenge to stay positive and not let the lack of progress defeat us, while also being aware that we were using excessive amounts of energy to cover small distances.

Occasionally, we were able to put on our skis, but that didn't make things any easier. Any brief downhill sections were a relief, although now I had to remember to step sideways in my skis at the right time so the sled sliding behind me wouldn't take me out. It became a work of art.

One of my biggest struggles from the North Pole had also come back to haunt me: my nose tends to dry out in the cold and I suffer a lot of nosebleeds. Anyone who has ever had them knows they are a pain and hard to stop. Plus, my neck had gotten very badly sunburned in the first couple of days and I had mild sunstroke – not what I was expecting to experience in a polar environment!

When we arrived at camp on the second night, we got out the GPS. With the weather as mild as it had been, we didn't need to rush to get the tents up. So I spread out my foam mat on the ice, took a seat and spent some time bonding with the team. We had been skiing for two days and, as the crow flew, we'd covered only 4.56 kilometres of our route, but had also reached an altitude of 711 metres. Considering our pre-trip plan was to average about 20 kilometres each day for the whole trip, we had some *serious* catching up to do. On the other hand, we could never have expected to travel those distances in the type of terrain we'd been covering. Plus, the mushy snow from the warm weather made the sleds even heavier to drag. During the day, we'd passed another team who had set off at the same time as us but had stopped for the night quite a way back. It made me think we were doing okay. Luckily, Eric felt the same way and had no concerns about the slow going as yet.

By the end of day three we had only covered around 20 kilometres of the 550-kilometre route and I was physically and emotionally shattered. Dad and I had also been bickering in the tent, trying to establish routines as teammates, rather than father and daughter.

You experience a lot of complex emotions when you're in this type of environment and under a large amount of physical and mental stress. There was no denying it would all become simpler once we'd got our days mapped out and our routines established again. We were still up to 27 days from the finish, but I'd already started counting down the days until we'd be heading home. At the same time, I felt blessed to be here in this magical place. As I said, all the feels become messed up and emotions are always changing.

The weather turned overcast, making visibility difficult. When the land is flat and white and the clouds extend all the way to the horizon, it feels quite eerie – as if you are skiing into oblivion. The dark lenses in our glacier sunglasses and goggles didn't help, but you couldn't remove them without risking snow blindness, caused by the glare of the snow.

When out front in these conditions, I'd try to pick a feature or outcrop in the distance that was also on our bearing and just ski towards it. We also had an old-school compass and the GPS with us, so we could be sure we were heading in the right direction. Most of the time we skied single file and I just put my headphones in and zoned out. Eric, Fred and Heath often did the same. In the rush to get ready, with work commitments and last-minute running around, Dad had accidentally left his headphones at home, so he was forced to be alone with his thoughts – something he said he quite enjoyed.

Our pattern each day was to ski for an hour then have a quick drink, followed by another hour of skiing, then a snack break, then ski–drink–ski–lunch–ski–drink–ski–snack–ski–drink–ski–camp. That meant around eight hours of skiing in total daily.

Halfway through the day, we would stop and have some lunch. As we were enjoying our noodles and frozen salami on the third day, we spotted the other group – 11 of them – pass us in the distance.

Eric had done this trip only once before, using a kite, and that had been 22 years ago, beginning in the opposite direction. He said back then it had felt as though he and his team had the entire Greenland ice sheet to themselves. Now, he said, we should expect to see another team in the distance at least twice during our travels.

By the end of the day the temperature had dropped quite a lot, making it easier to keep pushing, but I was suffering from a few new aches and pains. I'd managed to fall over a few times and, because it was warm and I was skiing with my gloves off, I had a few cuts on my hands from landing on the sharp ice, and they were also really sunburned.

At the other end, my feet were feeling marginally better now that we were on the skis. The even better news was that we'd managed to cover 15 kilometres during the day, so we all felt we'd achieved a lot.

❄

Each day out here had its own challenges. On day four, the GPS route Eric had been given by his friend, who had made the crossing many times before, suggested we take a route that included a dogleg because, supposedly, there was a crevasse field and a large section of open water on the direct path. But we couldn't see anything that looked menacing on the horizon so we decided to take a risk and press on in a straight line.

We came across no crevasses and no large melts, so at the end of our usual day, we were feeling good and decided to keep going until we hit the 20-kilometre mark. It was a great milestone for all of us. We'd managed to cover our full target distance for the first time since leaving Kangerlussuaq, and mentally it was just what I needed.

The next few days varied from great to ordinary. Dad and I were getting along well now that we had settled into our evening and morning routines in the tent. The terrain was flat, though all uphill — but the ascent was gradual, at least, so I eventually got used to the slow grind. The surface regularly switched from soft (which is much harder to ski on and makes the sled feel heavier) to hard (which makes life a lot easier) as we moved along. I listened to music to help pass the long hours while skiing, and Heath taught me how to navigate using a compass, the position of the sun and my shadow. The days are long out on the ice and just about any distraction is welcome. Once a day, I took a turn at leading the team and it was my favourite time.

As we got higher on the plateau, the temperature cooled right down and a headwind picked up, so we were back in our big jackets. Hypothermia and frostbite are real threats when the wind is blowing straight at your face.

I made an interesting discovery in those early days of the trip, too. Apparently, we didn't need to be as fanatical with our ice melting and water management as we had been in the North Pole. Due to the warmer weather, we could melt enough ice in the evening for our needs the next day and leave it in the kettle without it freezing solid overnight. After day eight, when we managed to cover our goal of 20 kilometres in record time, I woke very dehydrated. While we were no longer sweating much, we were losing lots of moisture through our breath. We needed to be drinking at least three litres of water a day, as well as hot drinks in the morning and the evening. Any less, and it was easy to become dangerously dehydrated.

All the same niggles – the ones we'd all had trouble with crossing the North Pole – cropped up early. My right hip flexor tended to tighten up, particularly towards the end of each day, one of my knees was playing up, my face and hands were windburned, and both Dad and I had pretty large and growing blisters on our feet.

It was also a long way to the nearest shower. We were still about 470 kilometres from our destination, and I already felt incredibly grotty. A wet wipe might cut it when you're camping out for a few nights, but when you start talking a few weeks they soon become inadequate. Something else new to me was the dead, flaky skin I was shedding (which I found out later is happening to everyone all the time, it's just that it's usually washed away when we shower and towel dry). When I changed clothes there was always a flurry of skin flakes in the tent. It was quite entertaining (at first).

As much as I was craving a shower, I was missing home-cooked meals even more – and, of course, missing home itself. A call to wish Mum a happy Mother's Day lifted my mood. She told me loads of people were leaving messages on my Instagram, which I updated once a day via satellite phone. It was easy to forget people knew where we were and worried about how we were doing, so hearing there was so much support from friends and even from people I'd never met was real motivation.

As we crawled out of our tents on day 10, I was confronted with my first true Arctic blizzard. But, far from daunted, I actually felt it was one of the coolest things I'd ever seen. The clouds merged with the horizon and there was no visible sun. Everything was white. The wind was strong and the snow was heavy, but the temperature was still quite warm. Unfortunately, though, the conditions quickly deteriorated.

During our journey so far, I'd seen many indications of how climate change is affecting Greenland – ice melts, the recessed snowline at our starting point – but what was happening now was the ultimate proof. We were walking straight into a howling blizzard, high on the second largest ice cap on the planet, but it wasn't blustering snow anymore – it was pelting rain.

8
BLIZZARD DAYS

As we pushed through the storm, the layers of our clothes became drenched. Polar gear is traditionally designed to keep you warm and shield against snow, but heavy rain is a completely different story. We hadn't contemplated this scenario when we were composing our gear list.

We had to make camp early when the rain became too intense, working together to get the tents up one at a time so nothing blew away into the endless horizon. Once the tent was up, Dad and I threw everything from our sleds into it from one side, then jumped in and sat in silence in our soaking gear until we had enough energy to speak and eventually strip off our saturated clothes. Once stripped off, we hung up our cold and wet clothes, which hadn't seen a washing machine in almost two weeks, on the makeshift clothes line inside. The fur ruffs on our polar shells shielded our faces from the wind like magic, but when they became wet, they reeked like the stench from a wet dog.

With all our wet clothes hanging above our heads, there was a rich aroma from the damp socks, musty thermals and polar outerwear just inches from my face as I ate my freeze-dried lamb fettuccine and hot Milo for dinner. It wasn't exactly pleasant. But for now, it was home and we were protected from the storm raging outside the thin walls of the tent.

We woke up the next day at the normal time of 6 am to the wind smashing the tent all around us and to find our sleds buried in snowdrift. Eric described the conditions as 'diabolically worse' than the day before and, by yelling between the tents, he told us to get comfy – it was too dangerous to go anywhere.

The big question, of course, was how to pass hours and hours trapped inside a tent. I'd never been stuck in a tent on an expedition before, so this was another level again. It was actually pretty exciting and surreal. I could have been at home doing schoolwork in my room, but instead I was in the middle of the Greenland ice cap, snowed in.

I had a Kindle, my diary, phone and music with me, so I had plenty of distractions, but I decided to take a nap instead.

I woke up to Eric yelling another update. If it was a couple of degrees colder, the rain would turn into snow and we'd be able to push on, since it wouldn't make our clothes wet.

The outsides of the tents were now soaked, which meant our clothes would be too if we tried to keep moving. And we hadn't brought wet weather gear because in all his years of polar travel Eric had never needed it. It felt more than a little bizarre to be in Greenland hoping for the temperatures to drop.

Eric had heard over the satellite phone that the other team who'd started at the same time as us had already made it a fair way further than we had, but were also sitting tight in their tents for the time being. They had apparently only brought 25 days' worth of food and fuel for the crossing, while we had brought enough for 30, so they were under extra time pressure. They'd also called for an evacuation when the weather cleared and were sending a few people who weren't coping with the conditions back to civilisation. When Eric enquired over the satellite phone what the issue was, he was told they had 'cold feet' – this is apparently the code that the guides use to describe clients who had minor issues like blisters but wanted to quit. Eric seemed to think we were in far better shape than them and he didn't seem even a bit worried that we'd had to take an enforced break.

I was actually feeling pretty positive about where we were at. It made me quite proud to know that I was pushing through while adults doing the same job were calling it quits. Of course, it was tough and I was feeling totally exhausted, but I knew this was the perfect training, physically and emotionally, for our South Pole expedition, which was now just seven months away.

We needed a decent break in the storm before we could pack up the camp and move on and we finally got that at about 2 pm. Everyone was settled into their sleeping bags, resting, reading or listening to music. Dad was outside building a toilet for me as a surprise – one with walls made from blocks of ice for privacy. After an hour or so I could hear him talking to Eric through the walls of the tent. I poked my head outside to find the weather had cleared and I could now see the horizon. Eric thought we should stay put and Dad was trying to convince him to get out of his comfy sleeping bag and come outside to take a look. Heath emerged first and confirmed Dad's assessment. Then Eric came out and agreed the weather seemed to have cleared, so we pulled everything down, packed up the sleds and moved on.

One thing that I learned is crucial in these conditions is knowing how to be comfortable with being uncomfortable. I do this by trying to focus on one thing in the present specifically. If I'm feeling cold or some part of my body is in pain, I direct all my thoughts to moving one foot in front of the other. I watch the skis moving in front of me and observe where my ski poles are breaking the surface of the ice. While it doesn't stop the cold or the pain, it shifts most of the focus. It also means we push on even when the conditions are far from perfect. We managed to get five hours of skiing in that day and covered 11 kilometres before we had to stop and set up camp. By 10 pm, we were back in our tents again, ready for another night.

Now the storm seemed to have gone, but dark clouds still threatened on the horizon, almost like some apocalypse slowly chasing us. We were well on our way to reaching DYE-2, one of the early-warning spy stations built by the USA on the Greenland ice cap during the Cold War to detect Russian missiles. Despite the less-than-ideal conditions, we still planned to reach the decommissioned site the next day, our eleventh on the trip. Then, according to our estimations, it would be another four days to reach the peak of the ice cap at about 2500 metres above sea level. The thought of heading downhill was pretty enticing. I was really looking forward to this – even some flat ground was much more appealing than the constant uphill slog.

One thing that became very clear to me during those tough days was the strength of my friendship with Heath Jamieson, the assistant to the camerawoman on our trip. A former special forces soldier in the Australian army, Heath had been through much more in his life than most of us could ever imagine and endured much tougher battles than skiing across this frozen island. He'd completed three tours of Afghanistan and had been shot through the neck, the bullet severing part of his spine and leaving him unable to walk. In 2013, he was part of the Walking with the Wounded expedition to the South Pole with Prince Harry. The fact that he was here with us and dragging the heaviest sled of all, full of all the camera gear we needed to make the documentary, was beyond extraordinary and it motivated me every day. I 100 per cent wanted him to come with us on the South Pole journey, no matter what.

I had very quickly discovered how much of a legend Heath is – he seems to have no issues with anything and has a knack for lightening the mood when it's required. He's the sort of person you are incredibly lucky to have alongside you on an expedition like this – selfless, knowledgeable and with a good sense of humour. He'd already taught me things I didn't even know were possible, like mind tricks he used to push through tough situations. When I got frustrated or cold and was at a low point, one of the first things he suggested was just to smile or laugh to myself. I soon realised that you can't feel bad when you do this! Another way he suggested to fight the pain was to take myself to another place, and focus only on the movement of skiing in my subconscious. He also taught me to clear my mind of any thoughts. I found this really hard to do, but once I nailed it, it made it so much easier to clear my mind of negative thoughts. It was almost like a meditation, and it was great to practise it out there, considering I often don't have time at home.

Good posture helped too, he said, and it worked. Standing tall and strong made my body believe that I was winning over the pain I was fighting. I felt as though I was growing and learning something new and priceless every day I spent with Heath. Eric was my guide and he was very professional, but Heath, without ever being asked, became my mentor. I learned more from him on my polar journeys than anyone or anything else. I will be forever grateful that I had Heath by my side on my toughest days.

In planning this trip, I had aimed to arrive in Tasiilaq on Greenland's East coast with enough time to interview some of the Inuit people, whose families have lived here for generations, as I was curious to learn about and understand their views on climate change. The weather continued to play havoc with our schedule, jeopardising this unique opportunity – especially when we woke to another 'Guys, we're not moving this morning' from Eric. Again, he had assessed the conditions and found them to be inhospitable and unsafe.

Sitting in the tent once more and knowing that we still had over 400 kilometres to go was frustrating beyond belief, and for a moment the thought did enter my mind that we might not get to the other side. To fail to make it to the east coast after two weeks of hard work and years of preparation earlier, would have been heartbreaking, so I was really keen to get moving as soon as we could.

Dad and I used the time to talk about the plans we'd made and what alternative plans might be required. Our projected arrival day became 4 June, the day before my sixteenth birthday. We had enough food to last until 7 June, but that was the day after Dad and I were due to fly home. It would probably mean I wouldn't get to conduct any interviews in Tasiilaq, but my main priority was getting there.

I had everything crossed that the wind would drop off and we could get out of the tents and continue our journey, so I was overjoyed when the weather cleared slightly at 4 pm. We could see DYE-2 in the distance, about 17.5 kilometres away, and I just wanted to get moving.

Slowly, we were chipping away at our goals, both the short-term goals and the ultimate one. In the end, we didn't make DYE-2 that night — we only had four hours of skiing time, during which we covered almost 13 kilometres — but I had new hope that we could get back on track.

❄

Heath taught me that the human brain is lazy. It wants to find any way to get out of hard work or being uncomfortable. I just needed to control my thoughts. It came in handy when I woke up feeling a little unwell.

The first hour of the day was a massive struggle for me mentally for a reason I couldn't grasp. It took all the tricks I'd learned from Heath to get myself back on track.

At some stage later in the session my nose started to bleed again. Some days out on the ice were better than others, and this was not shaping up to be a good one. Dad and I were skiing together behind, and everyone else was a long way in front. We had to pause and look for toilet paper to deal with the blood gushing from my nose. The guys in front stopped and waited. They were so far in front they couldn't see what we were doing. When we finally got moving again and caught up at the next break, they didn't bother to ask what had happened and why we'd stopped. I guess everyone was dealing with their own suffering at that point.

During the second session of the day, we made it to DYE-2. It was a really cool place, with a huge geodesic dome on its roof. It reminded me of the set of a science-fiction horror movie. The whole place had been trashed; all the windows had been smashed, there were drifts of snow inside and there was frozen leftover food everywhere. Apparently, when the US military abandoned the site in 1988, the workers just left most things where they were. Now, it was an interesting diversion for anyone skiing across the plateau and it looked as though plenty of people had stopped and sheltered here. We spent a couple of hours exploring the place with our head torches and Heath took the opportunity to sneak up on me through a side passage. I almost ended up with frozen pee pants again.

Camped just outside the site was Bjorn, the guide for the other Norwegian group, and three of his team members. They'd made camp and were waiting to be evacuated. Another guide from the same team who had gone ahead was now heading back to join them with two additional people who also wanted to leave the expedition. It was disappointing for those who weren't going to make it, but it was an extra dose of motivation for me. I was still going.

As we left DYE-2 we encountered a nearby US military training camp called Camp Raven. Ski-equipped Hercules planes land and take off there on the ice runways as practice for when the American pilots have to fly scientists and other workers to and from Antarctica. There were also scientists working there, which led to a chance meeting with a German woman called Regine Hock, from the University of Alaska Fairbanks, who walked out of their camp to greet us as we skied past. She was studying glacier mass change and climate change, and was generous enough to spend some time telling me all about her findings and her thoughts on the changing climate.

Until I'd been on the ground in the North Pole and Greenland, I was slightly reluctant to believe that global warming was really happening and that it was having the kind of rapid effect on our world that scientists were claiming. But my first-hand experiences certainly opened my eyes to the truth. It is impossible to deny it when you're seeing it through your own eyes. In Greenland, the obliteration of the snowline back at Kanger-lussuaq, the melt ponds and the blizzard in which snow was replaced by rain, added to what I had learned from speaking to John at DMI and now Regine. This was all proof of just how much trouble these pristine and fragile environments are in. It made me want to learn as much as I can about the environmental impact of humans and what we can do to protect our planet and these amazing environments for future generations.

Eric was starting to get worried, and his frustration was beginning to show – he felt we were travelling too slowly and was keen for us to push harder.

According to him, being high up on the ice cap – we were at about 2000 metres at this stage – was excellent preparation and a great test for Antarctica. Our current trip was around 30 days and 550 kilometres; the new route we were planning from the coast to the South Pole would be close to 40 days out on the ice to cover around 600 kilometres in much tougher conditions.

Eric had already told me a bit about what we could expect in Antarctica. Much of the plateau there sits at about 3000 metres above sea level and it is a brutal and unforgiving place. The altitude combined with very low temperatures can make it extremely dangerous. Having that as my next goal helped me push through any doubts in Greenland. I had to completely conquer this otherwise our December trip would not be looking good.

At the end of day 14, we had only covered around 200 kilometres. We were halfway through our food and fuel and we still had 354 kilometres to go according to the GPS.

Dad and I redid the sums after dinner in our tent and came to the realisation that we were going to have to smash about 25 kilometres a day for the rest of the trip, assuming no more weather delays, to make the coast by the day before I turned 16 – this would be day 27.

That night, Dad and I made a commitment to each other that we would make this happen. We would give it everything, no matter how tough it got and even though I had a list of complaints and injuries as long as my aching arms. We had our goal.

The self-imposed pressure was good; we skied faster and added an extra hour to the next two days and managed to cover 24.5 kilometres and 25.5 kilometres. The extra hour of skiing a day meant getting the eight hours' sleep each night (generally from 10 pm to 6 am) required to recover properly was a real challenge. I usually wasn't getting to sleep before 11 pm each night anyway. We spent that extra hour of skiing moving closer to our goal, but there were lots of other things to be done every day too – setting up camp, melting ice for water, having dinner, writing in my journal and filming video diaries for the Nat Geo documentary – and time just always seemed to get away.

The halfway point was approaching so quickly. For the most part, I was spending quite a bit of time skiing on my own. At other times, particularly when frustration was kicking in, I'd ski with Heath. Seemingly small things tended to get on my nerves (and everyone else's) in these conditions. One of the main culprits, again, was going to the toilet. Back home, I take it for granted, but when the landscape becomes flat, there's nowhere to hide.

We tried stacking a couple of the sleds for me to shelter behind, but that also took extra time, and the delays were driving Eric crazy. He was mad and after one stop gave me a lecture about how I needed to speed up my toilet breaks. This really frustrated me and so I decided to head off in front with Heath, who was leading during the next session.

There's nothing like keeping up with a speed demon to work out the negative emotions. Each time Heath turned around I was right on his tail. I kept up with him, despite him being 190 centimetres tall and standing head and shoulders above me.

When the two of us stopped for a quick break, Heath turned to me and said, 'Frustrations are sometimes good.' I felt as though he understood what I was feeling. We certainly think many of the same things. I told him about what had happened at the last break and why I was angry, and he pointed to his chest and told me that was where I found my strength. I felt myself thriving when he gave me motivation, even if it was only a few words.

It made me take a deep breath and have a chat to Dad later that day after we'd set up camp. We decided between ourselves to focus only on what we needed to do to achieve our goal – not to be distracted by others – to be ourselves and, importantly, to move at our own pace and not worry so much about the pressure to ski faster. If it meant long days, we didn't mind.

By day 16 we'd made it to an altitude of 2500 metres, near the summit of the Greenland ice cap. What an achievement.

And while it took a few more days of undulating ups and downs, it eventually became downhill from there.

9
THE NEW NORMAL

'Morning!' Eric would yell out every morning at 6 am, which meant it was time to get up. Unfortunately, he didn't come with a snooze button. Dad would get straight up and start the stove. I would follow slowly, very slowly, not long after Dad to begin all the things that needed to be done before we could get skiing . . . as I mentioned, I am not a morning person.

First, the stove needed to be lit and the water put on the heat. In Greenland it was always still liquid from the night before, but if it wasn't hot in our drink bottles when we got going in the morning there was a chance it could freeze during the day. This was my cue to get up. Once the stove is going the worst part of the fumes from the flame hang around the bottom of the tent so there was no chance I was hanging around down there.

Each night, the last task before jumping in the tent would be for one of us to take our big blue IKEA bag and a shovel and cut blocks of ice in the snow. Once we'd cut enough blocks for water that fitted neatly in the kettle pot, we'd take them back to the tent and place them next to the stove. From there, we could melt them on the stove. It would take around three hours each evening to melt enough ice to provide water to rehydrate dinner as well as for a cup of hot Milo and our drinking water for the next day. At home, you take it for granted that you turn the tap and water comes out instantaneously, but in Greenland (in fact, in all polar environments) we really had to work for it.

Seventeen days in and I continued to put one ski in front of the other, fighting the pain of sore muscles and blisters. It was relentless and, at times, very monotonous. The name of the polar-crossing game was to take it one day at a time, rest, refuel and repeat.

Sometimes performing the same movement over and over again became frustrating, but most times I managed to lose myself in the motion, which seemed to make the hours pass much faster. When we stopped, though, it was apparent my body had been performing the same movement for hours on end. When I stretched, I could feel how sore all my muscles were. But there was no avoiding the aches and pains.

Because we'd hit 2500 metres above sea level, I had started to feel the altitude a little, too. The air is thinner the higher you go, so there's less oxygen to fuel the activity. I had periods of feeling incredibly light-headed – it was especially bad when I stood up suddenly or bent over to fix the bindings on my skis. I also had a couple more of my big nosebleeds. I knew they were caused by breathing in cold, dry air through my nose, but I'm pretty sure the altitude didn't help.

Eric was still worried about our progress. I was still having issues with privacy during toilet breaks, and he had issues with my need for privacy causing delays. I came up with the solution of stopping for my toilet break a few hundred metres before where everyone else was stopping for break. Then I would catch up and have my break. This seemed to work well, but it meant that in harsh conditions, my breaks were a lot more crammed than the guys'.

Eric's concerns about pace were justified, and I understood he was thinking forward to our Antarctica trip, which was only around six months away. It was going to be tougher and much longer, so I needed to be able to perform efficiently even when I wasn't feeling efficient. He wanted all of us to keep our fiddling – putting on mittens, getting headphones in our ears – to a minimum. It was a little hard to believe that 10 seconds here and 30 seconds there would make that much difference to our progress, but Eric had done a huge number of these expeditions, so I took his advice and tried harder.

It had been a pretty rough few days and I was feeling quite low emotionally as we reached the highest geographical point of the whole journey. It helped to take a few moments to remember the enormity of what we'd achieved already, climbing upwards for 300 kilometres.

To make it to the coast in 27 days still looked remotely possible, but we'd need everything to go right from here. No bad weather, no injuries and everyone giving it their best shot. But conditions were still not great – visibility was very low and, although we tried to stick to a straight course, in a white-out the lead person would snake around, often having to turn behind them to use the line of our single-file team to understand if they were heading straight or not.

Plus, unbelievably, the weather just kept getting warmer. The temperatures of around 0°C were the same as those we'd encountered when we started on the coast. We were wearing caps to protect our faces from the sun and often ended up stripping right down to our thermals. The worst bit was sweating while we were moving along. If there was even a little bit of wind, it was so painful when we stopped – the moisture would chill almost instantly and we'd end up freezing cold, making it even harder to get moving again. At breaks we'd need to slather ourselves in sunscreen. It was also making the going very heavy in the slushy ice. Add the melting effects of the sun's rays with the fact we'd had a bit of snowfall over the previous few days and it made for hard work moving those skis and dragging the sleds behind us.

Life on the ice had become the new normal for me by then and my previous life at home in Melbourne seemed as though it were a dream. Getting closer to being back there had made

me start to think of what I was going to do when I arrived. Of
course, first on the list was a hot shower that I was sure would
be the best shower of my life. A home-cooked meal was a close
second; I was thinking specifically of poached eggs and bacon.
In the tent that night I made a list of all the things I now realised
I take for granted at home. In no particular order, they were:

- running water
- Mum's home-cooked meals
- a shower and soap
- heaters
- a bed with pillows and a doona
- a toilet with a door
- internet
- electricity
- fresh milk
- clean clothes
- clean sheets
- clean smell
- darkness
- tables and chairs
- dry shoes
- family and friends
- cars and roads
- sleep
- a variety of foods.

I vowed I would never take them for granted again.

❄

Because mornings are my least favourite time of the day, I realised that I needed to turn this around, crank myself up and really go as hard as I could in the first two sessions. It worked, too. When I used that time to push myself, the rest of the day felt much easier. On day 18, we managed to cover a total of 26 kilometres, which was a new record for us. Dad gave me a hug to celebrate and, because he'd taken his skis off but I still had mine on, I was finally taller than him!

It was the following day when it really felt as though we were beginning to move downhill. Overnight the temperature had dropped to −20°C, and it felt like we were going to be able to move fast on the hard surface. In the first session, we covered almost four kilometres in just over an hour, which was a fantastic pace. The cold temperatures overnight made the ice solid and that really made a difference to how fast we could go. We hoped it was an omen for the rest of the trip.

Dad and Eric took the lead, with Fred keeping pace. Heath and I skied along together a short distance behind them. As we all came together during one break, Eric told us he could see the colours of our suits imprinted against the white background when he looked back over his shoulder, which was a sure sign we were really kicking in to the downhill. It couldn't have come at a better time. By then, Dad and I had really horrific blisters. One of mine ran right down the outside of my big toe all the way onto the ball of my foot. Dad had one on the bottom of his foot that just seemed to get bigger and more grotesque every day. There was no way he could adjust how he skied to put less pressure on it.

Whenever we'd feel a new hot spot or blister, we'd put some sports tape on it to stop the friction, and by then our feet were more plaster than skin. At night, we'd clean them with wet wipes to make sure they didn't get infected and then cover them again. There was no other way to describe it than absolutely disgusting. We'd followed our packing lists, which said we only needed four pairs of socks, and we were wearing through those pairs fast. And the insides of them were caked with the glue from the previous day's tape.

While the mornings were cool, the afternoons were insanely hot in the sun. We'd take our boots off during the lunch break. It was so weird to be sitting in the middle of Greenland with bare feet! Dad was skiing in a t-shirt with his polar shell pants rolled up to his knees, and I was getting head spins every time I stood up. Our feet were squelching inside our ski boots. I was craving a day at the beach. When I'd been psyching myself up for this trip, I never expected that the two biggest challenges would be rain and heat.

We were deep into day 20 when Heath said to me, 'There's no place I'd rather be right now.'

It was so true. Being immersed in nature on a grand scale with hardly any other humans gives you a feeling and a perspective you just can't explain. I felt as though I had forgotten my old life and become used to a new one and it would be this way forever. I wrote in my diary that night my new thoughts:

- Your limits are not your limits. There are no limits.
- You can't always control other people.
- So much is taken for granted.
- The mind is the most powerful tool.
- You can learn so much from other people by listening.
- Keep an open mind.
- Pain is temporary. Glory is forever.

Dad later explained to me that this last quote, which is famous, is a great one for pushing through discomfort, but it's wrong. The glory doesn't last forever and it's not what's important. What does last, and what is of true value, is what you learn from the pain and who you become from pushing through the suffering. The suffering wasn't something to avoid, but to relish as an opportunity to reinvent ourselves.

The unseasonal warmth meant we had some unexpected visitors. There was one little bird that decided it was going to follow us and would shelter near the sleds during our breaks, hoping for some crumbs. Occasionally we'd also see flocks of birds flying in formation just above the surface of the ice. It had been a while since we'd seen other living creatures apart from each other and it was a beautiful and freaky sight.

Even freakier were the huge polar bear tracks we came across on day 21. They were the tracks of a mother and her cub and, just like the tracks we'd seen on the North Pole trip, I could put my whole hand inside one of the mother's paw prints. Eric was surprised to see evidence of polar bears this far inland, and mentioned that their only sources of food here were us and the Norwegian team crossing at the same time. Dad joked that Australians are probably more of a delicacy in these parts than the Norwegians. He wasn't helping.

Both Eric and Heath thought the tracks may have been there for less than 12 hours, so we went into high alert. Of course, we had a firearm with us, but that was purely to scare the bear and would only have been used as a last resort. We were in the bear's territory, and if you get to the point where you have to fire a gun, you are in big trouble.

We were told that if a bear came anywhere near us, we should make a lot of noise by banging our ski poles into the ice or onto our sleds. It makes a similar noise to walruses banging their tusks on the ice to scare the bears away. We were also told to make ourselves look big and threatening by waving our poles in the air and jumping on top of our sleds. Loud, obnoxious noises were good, too. Dad told me that if we came across a bear I was to get behind him, as Mum had told him not to come home without me.

When we set up camp that night we also made a fairly basic early-bear-warning barrier that would hopefully wake us up if one entered the camp. Ski poles in the snow were made into corner posts and we strung rope between them. We then leaned our skis up against the rope, so that if a bear hit the rope during the night the clattering of skis would hopefully wake us up. Dad and I slept with a shovel and ice axe beside us, just in case . . .

We survived the night without the polar bears coming anywhere near us. We had been lucky. It was a pity we weren't having the same luck with the weather conditions. The heat continued to swelter. We were down at around 2000 metres above sea level now and it was only going to get warmer.

Every part of my body was so sore; my back was spasming, the blisters on my feet were getting worse and any part of my body that was exposed to the elements was sunburned – including the roof of my mouth – from the sun's reflection off the ice.

With only five days to go, I was also starting to worry that I had been wishing this expedition away. The trip to the North Pole had been and gone so quickly, it was over before I knew it. We'd been on the ice in Greenland for three weeks already and I wanted to make sure I took in every minute of it.

In the tent that night I opened one of the letters my best friends had given me – the last one left before we finished. My two best friends had written around 10 letters for me to open and read along the way as a bit of motivation. In this one were the lyrics to 'Ice Ice Baby' by Vanilla Ice, which I was challenged to learn before I finished the crossing. I thought it was hilarious. I missed my friends so much while I was away. I spent the rest of the night driving Dad mad trying to rap the words to the song on repeat.

We really had just one big push left to get to the end, but we were all struggling, including Frederique, who had a hacking cough. Eric had warned us we might need to have a rest day for Fred to recover. Dad, Heath and I did not want to take a rest day. Heath was having real trouble with his leg but he's insanely tough and I knew he would have rather crawled to the coast than slow everyone down. Stopping again would mean we definitely would not make it to the East coast by day 27 and we'd probably miss our flight home. We compromised with Eric and finished skiing a bit earlier on one day to give everyone a bit of a rest.

We had 72 kilometres to go to reach the ice fall and three days to get there. That meant we needed to cover 25 kilometres each day. It was a big ask, but on day 24 we smashed out 26.9 kilometres.

The mental exertion of the long expedition was messing with all of our heads. Long days of sameness meant there was nothing much else for my brain to do apart from run away on strange trains of thought. I would think about whether I was ever going to do anything that would make a real difference to help others. And if the world was going to end eventually anyway, what was the point in even trying? Luckily, each evening, I had Mum on the other end of the phone, and she reminded me that life is life and I just had to live mine as best I could and enjoy it.

The next couple of days were a blur. We were punching out the target distances, hitting all the goals Dad and I had set ourselves, and our strange moods came and went. Dad and I had a few clashes in the tent, but I knew we only had a little bit longer to keep it together. I was tired, but so was he. I made a pact with myself that I was going to dig deep to make the last days as emotionally painless as possible.

❄

We awoke on our last full day on the ice to one of the coolest things I've ever seen. It was windy and cold when we stepped out of the tent. The sun was visible but there were also puffs of low cloud sitting on the horizon. It looked almost like smoke from a distant bushfire. I turned my attention back to the tent we'd just packed up and within a matter of seconds the wind had stopped. I looked back at the cloud as it rushed towards us and immersed us in a white mist.

Heath explained that anabatic winds go uphill and katabatic winds go downhill. In this case, the katabatic winds were stronger than the anabatic ones and they were holding the cloud low on the horizon, but when the anabatic winds became stronger, the clouds basically flew over us and blocked out the sun. For quite a while we were walking into cloud and I quickly lost sight of Dad and Eric. I felt alone, but calm. Beams of light struck through openings in the clouds around me and it almost felt as if I was floating.

Once the cloud lifted, later in the day, it became incredibly hot and I could feel my racoon tan around my eyes getting even worse. We ended up on some quite steep downhill stretches, so we all got on our sleds and tobogganed down as best we could in the slushy ice. We could see the coastal mountains in the distance, over the dip of the horizon. It was a relief to see a feature on the landscape after spending weeks looking at nothing but endless plains of white.

It was the last night of the trip, and instead of rushing to set up my side of the tent as soon as we'd assembled it like normal, I sat outside on my sled in the warmth of the sun gazing over the mountains, the ocean and icebergs in the distance. It was honestly like something out of a movie. I just sat there for ages, thinking about nothing and losing myself in the moment.

We were only a day away.

We began our final day with a safety briefing from Eric on how to sit on our sleds and ride them down steeper sections like responsible adults (we'd gone a bit crazy the day before). He didn't want us to injure ourselves so close to the finish, so he showed us how to use the rope attached to our sleds as a brake, as well as how to turn the sled with our skis on the snow. 'Don't be afraid to bail out if you have to,' he said. 'And don't anyone fall into a crevasse. It's not good for my reputation.'

We took a long snack break overlooking the rocky shore that ran down to the ocean. We luged some of the bigger distances and covered them with speed. Eventually, we could see where the snow finished and where the rock started. Finally, our objective – Isortoq Hut, which marks the East coast and our end goal – came into view.

We had made it.

It's tradition to touch a rock on the coast when you arrive, so I detached from my sled, took off my skis, headed for the biggest boulder I could see and climbed up on top. When I turned to face the others, I threw my hands in the air and started laughing. We all hugged and celebrated. Eric called the pilot of the helicopter to make sure it was on its way. The pilot told us he'd be about 90 minutes.

We had a mini debrief while waiting. Eric was now assured we were going to be fine in Antarctica – that I would lap it up, love it and nail it.

I hoped so too, although it felt strange to already be talking about Antarctica when we'd only just finished Greenland.

We walked up to the little wooden Isortoq Hut and took some photos, including one with our family's Australian flag, which is a tradition on all our family adventures.

We soon heard the approaching roar of a helicopter. It was quite little and red and, when its blades finally stopped, Tim, the pilot, climbed out. He took one look at the sleds and told us there was no way we'd fit everything in the chopper. What?! We spent an hour or so trying to solve the puzzle, but the pilot's assessment was right.

In the end, all the sleds had to stay behind with Eric and Heath to wait for a bigger helicopter, while Dad, myself and Fred took a small portion of our personal gear and flew out to Tasiilaq for our scheduled interviews for the Nat Geo documentary with local Inuit people the day after. A lot of work had gone into setting up this unique opportunity to listen to their perspective on global warming and I didn't want to miss it.

At our starting point on the West coast of Greenland, we carried our sleds, one by one, to where the ice had retreated.

In the early part of our Greenland crossing the weather was so warm that we got a lot of our drinking water from the ice melts without having to use the stove.

Working our way through the maze of the West coast ice fall.

Stuck in the tent trying to dry all our gear after getting caught in a rain blizzard.

Trying to stay ahead of the blizzard.

Low cloud on the Greenland plateau.

Approaching the abandoned US spy station (DYE-2) in the middle of Greenland.

Signing the visitors' book at DYE-2. The station is full of junk that was left behind when the US abandoned the station in October 1988.

Opening a letter from Zoe. These letters from my best friends, Zoe and Mia, were always a laugh.

Lunchtime in Greenland. This was the only time during each day that we removed our skis.

High on the Greenland plateau.

Buff pulled high, headphones in and wearing only liner mitts – a warm weather expedition kit.

One of our camps in the West coast ice fall.

Dad and me holding our family flag at the Greenland expedition finishing point –
Isortoq Hut on the East coast. Check out the raccoon tan!

Nevertheless, it was really weird being separated from the rest of the team – for the last four weeks, we had only had each other. Now the transition back to the real world had begun.

10
THE BLUR BETWEEN

It definitely wasn't the sixteenth birthday I'd imagined. Back in Tasiilaq, we stayed in the only lodge in town. A shower was the best thing ever and it was a treat to have my own tiny bedroom and not to have to sleep in a tent with Dad for the first time in 27 days.

In the morning, we raided the common kitchen at the lodge. All we could find was some stale cereal and warm milk. That was breakfast. Afterwards, Dad gave me some birthday cards from family back home and a little gift-wrapped present from him of a Coco Pops-flavoured lip balm, which he'd carried all the way across Greenland for my birthday.

Thankfully, we were back in time to be able to finish this

trip the way I'd hoped: with the time to interview some of the local Inuit people about their perspectives on climate change for the documentary being made for National Geographic. I felt very privileged to have these conversations.

They told me that warmer weather is impacting on their traditional way of life as hunters – this part of their culture is slowly disappearing along with the ice – but in a lot of other ways it might be a positive (I wasn't convinced they were feeling very positive about it, though). Warmer temperatures in Greenland mean the ice is retreating, revealing a wealth of underground resources that could be mined, and crops would be easier to grow. Mining and agriculture would also mean jobs for many of the locals who don't have them currently.

Later that day, Dad and I flew out to Reykjavik in Iceland, where we were planning to celebrate my birthday properly. Villa, who I had met on my trek to Everest Base Camp and who had inspired my polar journeys, was living in Reykjavik at the time and she'd just returned from summitting Everest. We met up with her at the Blue Lagoon, a man-made lagoon in a lava field. We had dinner at the restaurant there, then swam in the geothermal spas until about midnight, when the sun set. It was incredible, and Villa gave me a really beautiful necklace to wear and keep me safe on my South Pole expedition at the end of the year. It was barely six months away, and just a couple days after finishing Greenland, I was already eager to get started on our preparation.

We arrived back in Melbourne and hit the ground running, despite jetlag. I had four days of media commitments before we were back on a plane to Washington DC for my second Nat Geo Explorers Festival.

It was a huge couple of days at Nat Geo headquarters, where I networked with many people from Nat Geo and heard researchers and scientists speak about their recent discoveries and future projects. The theme of that year's conference was Red Planet vs Blue Planet, and the discussion was focused on whether humans should be investing so much into trying to colonise other planets, like Mars, or whether we should be exploring Earth's largely unexplored oceans. One speaker said the total budget for exploring Earth's oceans each year is equivalent to the cost of just a one-way trip for one astronaut into outer space. I was amazed to hear that we know more about the moon's surface than we do about the deepest parts of Earth's oceans.

For me, the highlight of the program was attending a session featuring the famous astrophysicist Neil deGrasse Tyson and James Cameron, the director of *Avatar* and *Titanic* and a deep-sea explorer himelf. From opposing sides, they discussed taking exploration in completely different directions – into space or into the oceans – to accommodate our exploding population growth.

Another inspiring speaker we heard from was Bob Ballard, a retired US Navy officer, National Geographic Explorer and the person who found the wreck of the *Titanic* in 1985. He spends five months of the year exploring the oceans' deepest points.

His solution to saving the environment is one I'm also very passionate about: empowering women. He's an advocate of micro-loans to women in third world countries, so they can create small businesses and offer something to their communities.

I also took special interest in the discussion about Enceladus, the sixth-largest moon of Saturn, which is mostly covered by frozen fresh water. It also contains an underground ocean. Many believe it is our best chance of finding another habitable world in our solar system and by all means, there could be life there already. But the only way to find out for sure would be to send a spacecraft there. Enceladus's surface temperature sits at around −200°C, which is next level.

By the time I returned to Melbourne, I had been away for almost two months, and Antarctica was already looming.

Eric had told me he thought I was ready to take on this massive expedition, but I didn't want to develop a big head and take the pressure off myself. We only had five months to go and I knew I still had a lot of work to do. Training for this trip would be similar to the previous two, however this trip would be a lot longer in distance and time, so we planned on doing some more longer-distance, endurance training sessions, such as dragging car tyres behind us (wearing our polar harnesses) on sandy beaches for hours without rest.

It was to be the finale of the Polar Hat-Trick and my polar journey.

THE
SOUTH
POLE

EXPEDITION 3

Destination: The South Pole

Distance: 600 kilometres

Duration: 37 days, December 2017–January 2018

Goal: To ski a new route from the coast (Ross Ice Shelf) to the South Pole. To be the youngest person in history (male or female) to ski from the coast to the South Pole unsupported and unassisted

Team: Me, Dad, Eric, cameraman Ming D'Arcy, Heath

Big challenges: Some of the toughest weather conditions in Antarctica in many years, uncertainty of exploring a new route to the Pole, sastrugi, crevasse fields

Everyday challenges: Spotify failing after the first week (over 300 hours of skiing without music), temperatures as low as –50°C with windchill, pain

11
PREPPING IN PUNTA

It was December 2017, and we had arrived in Punta Arenas, in the southernmost region of Chile, to organise last-minute preparations for my biggest expedition yet. It had been a long time travelling from Melbourne to Punta Arenas – about 17 hours in all. Unfortunately, even though Antarctica is so close to Melbourne direct, the only way to enter mainland Antarctica by plane for expeditions is via Chile, halfway around the world. Now, we had a few days to recover from jetlag and get ourselves organised. Our team – Eric, Dad, Heath, myself and Ming D'Arcy (our new Nat Geo cameraman for this expedition) – spent a couple of days working in a big warehouse getting ready for 40 days in Antarctica.

Everything was checked over to make sure it was in good working order (we didn't want to discover a stove wasn't working out on the ice), then checked off again before it was packed. Our gear list was huge, despite the efforts for minimal weight.

We had everything required plus some extras as contingency plans. We needed stoves to make dinner in the tent at night, but we also needed a stove repair kit. We packed extra skis and ski poles, just in case any got lost or broken. Even simple things, like matches – forget those and your journey is over before it even starts. If you can't light your stoves while you're out on the ice, you won't survive.

Eric had sent a gear list to Dad and me in Melbourne months earlier, and in the lead-up to this trip, we'd been sorting out our gear and piling it up on the floor at home. The final gear list was similar to the one we followed in Greenland. It had been comparatively warm there and most of the layers were never even used. But over the coming weeks, we were going to be enduring some of the coldest winds on the planet. I expected to be wearing every layer I had with me.

In a quiet moment in the Punta warehouse, Dad dobbed me in. 'Jade may have brought a few things that aren't on the list,' he said, always looking for a chance to stir the pot. He then revealed to Eric that I'd packed 20 pairs of underpants. It really didn't sound at all excessive to me for a trip that was going to last 40 days, but the gear list specified three and Eric was only taking two! Two pairs of undies for almost six weeks is plain *gross*! It didn't get any better. Dad confessed to bringing just four pairs, and I was sharing a tent with him. Apparently, Eric wears them inside out and back to front, so he reckons he's got four pairs in one. I'm not even sure he's done the maths right on this.

'You throw them out at the end though, right?' I asked.

Eric looked at me as if I'd just suggested he wear them on his head. 'No. They're perfectly fine after you give them a wash.'

Then he threatened to trade some of my chocolate in for every extra pair of undies I had in my bag. It wasn't going to happen. I was taking those knickers, and *no one* gets between me and my chocolate.

Again, our expedition was unsupported and unassisted, which meant we had to take everything we needed on our sleds. There would be no resupplies by air, which is now the most common approach for full-distance coast-to-Pole expeditions. We weren't able to use motorised transport, kites or dogs to make life easier, and we weren't permitted to follow any sort of road or track that had been made by a vehicle. This should give you some idea of why checking off the gear list is so important . . .

And while we couldn't afford to leave anything behind, at the same time we didn't want to take anything superfluous, not only because there are weight limits on the flights from Punta Arenas to the start point, but because we were going to have to pull those sleds for 40 days up a glacier then across the Antarctic Plateau to the South Pole. The heavier the sleds, the slower we would go, and there was definitely a finite amount of time in which to complete the whole expedition. The sleds were already going to be heavy enough. On our first trip, to the North Pole, my sled weighed about 60 kilograms at the start. It started off at about 75 kilograms when we crossed Greenland, but this time around my sled would be around 100 kilograms at the beginning. This was heavy. Because we were attempting a new route through the Transantarctic Mountains, just as Amundsen and Scott had done 106 years earlier, we needed equipment that an expedition following the traditional route from Hercules Inlet would not need, such as crampons, long ropes, carabiners, harnesses and crevasse rescue equipment.

In addition, I was carrying a few extra kilos myself. In preparation for this trip, Dad had encouraged me to gain some extra weight, as he assured me I would lose plenty from the hard work of dragging the heavy sled and my body simply trying to keep itself warm. I normally weigh around 58 kilograms, but as I stood there in Punta, I was 64.5 kilos! I had eaten a lot of ice-cream to get to that point – when I sat down I had to undo the top button on my jeans.

It was the perfect example of why young women need to shift their focus from how they appear to the possibilities of what they can do: I needed to build a body that was strong, and carrying extra weight was the best way to do that.

Just before I left home I did a fashion shoot and interview for *Vogue* magazine that appeared in the March 2018 issue. I was pretty sure I would be the only person in that issue with a double chin.

During this expedition, we would be attempting the first-ever ascent of the Kansas Glacier, which I imagined would be so surreal. For me, doing these expeditions was never about records; what really excited me was the adventure and, now, true exploration. Fewer than 1 per cent of people who ski from the coast to the South Pole follow a new route, so this was going to be an incredible privilege.

The difference between the North Pole and the South is that here we were guaranteed to be moving over and between crevasses.

I started competing in triathlons when I was seven years old. I was terrified of swimming in the open ocean and, for many years, I would swim with my eyes closed. But now, falling into a bottomless crevasse was my biggest fear. As opposed to the traditional route to the Pole, where all crevasse dangers are marked with GPS coordinates, all we had was an old map and aerial photographs from the 1960s. As we'd be the first people to move through this area on the ground, we would have to feel our way and take precautions when unsure. But I had to block my fears out of my mind and focus on the job at hand. I knew I could get myself out of a crevasse if I had to – I'd done it in New Zealand. But I really hoped I wasn't tested like that.

One of my biggest tasks pre-Antarctica was to organise the food. After two polar expeditions, I felt like I knew what I was doing. We were thankfully taking Eric's breakfast bomb with us once again. Like my mum always said: breakfast is the most important meal of the day; out on the ice this was especially the case. Eric's mix was packed with so much we needed – oats,

milk powder, protein powder, desiccated coconut and pecans –
to get the day started and fill us up until we took our first
snack break.

There were so many zip-lock bags to be filled – one for
every day of the expedition. Into each one I packaged a nut mix
(I often saved mine for near the end of the day because it filled
me up and gave me a final boost), five crackers, two muesli
bars, 50 grams each of cheese, salami and butter, dehydrated
noodles with either organic chicken or beef broth, and one
whole block of chocolate – the chocolate was my favourite part
of the food bag by a long shot. Before I put all the items into the
bags, I removed the external packaging and wrappers so that
we didn't create any extra rubbish that we'd have to carry with
us to the Pole.

Our dinners, which were freeze-dried, were packed separ-
ately. There was a good range of flavours, like chicken masala
and spaghetti bolognese. Each meal packet served two, so there
was always some discussion between Dad and I about what
meal we would have at the end of each day.

It might seem like an intense amount of food, but we
really had to ensure we were consuming enough calories for
our bodies to be able to cope with the extreme activity and
temperatures. One of the worst things that could happen was
running out of rations. There's no coming back from that –
we would have to be evacuated. The only way I could see us
running out of food was if we were snowed in for a long time.
And even if that happened we could cut our rations to eke out
an extra few days.

All up, there was one kilogram of food per person each day, so for each of us that was more than 40 kilograms of food alone we were dragging on our sleds. The upside was that each day the sled got a kilo lighter. Added to that weight was the fuel we had to carry for the stove. Much of the weight in our sleds was just about basic survival requirements – food and water.

While we were preparing, Antarctic Logistics & Expeditions (ALE), the company that manages all logistics and flights internally in Antarctica, posted on their Instagram that the driest continent on Earth was dropping some uncharacteristically wet, heavy snow on Union Glacier. It sounded a lot like the wet storm that had hit us while we were in Greenland. Perhaps it's something we'll see more of as climate change becomes more pronounced. We still had a few days to go before we flew out, and even though we hadn't had much luck with the starts to our previous expeditions, we hoped that conditions would soon clear.

We assembled for a briefing at ALE's offices in Punta with everyone else who would be on our flight. They gave us an indication of the weather in Antarctica and how likely it was that we'd actually leave the next day, 4 December, as planned. The weather can change very quickly in Antarctica, and it's not safe for planes to land on the blue ice runway when conditions are bad. Sometimes they boomerang – that is, they get to the landing area, decide it's too windy, and turn around and go back. Luckily, there is excellent forecasting these days, so once our plane had taken off from Punta Arenas there was a better likelihood it would be able to land in Antarctica.

At the briefing, ALE director Mike Sharp told us the Russian Ilyushin aircraft we would be flying on was already being loaded and the weather was looking promising for our departure the following day. The company had some other groups heading off – 10 people were going to see the emperor penguins, and another group was driving six-wheel Toyota Hiluxes from the coast to the Pole along an ice road. On our flight were also three glaciologists from Valdivia, who were investigating a lake that had formed three kilometres below the ice, some people skiing the last degree and a number of ALE staff. One of them was Daniel, ALE's meteorologist who specialises in Antarctica. I asked him lots of questions about climate change. He told me many people don't realise Antarctica actually drives most of the world's climates – the melting ice on the fringes of the continent pushes all of the world's ocean currents around and they have a big effect on the climate everywhere.

Recently it had been discovered there was a lot of melting going on beneath the ice. It couldn't be seen, but many scientists were redirecting their research to observe the occurrence. It could be having a huge effect, as it eats into the underneath of the ice, increasing the rate at which the ice flows off the continent.

Daniel also mentioned that people were beginning to question whether global warming was real because there had been 'record sea ice coverage in Antarctica'. Unfortunately, no one really knows how thick that sea ice was in the past. There had been some recent research into the depth of the ice and it proved that although the coverage is greater, it didn't contain the same volume of ice. Much like in the North Pole, there had also been greater variability in conditions, so things were changing, even if no one was entirely sure what was going on. To me, such huge changes in conditions reinforce why addressing climate change needs to be made a major priority for governments around the world.

When the briefing was over, Eric found a map of Antarctica on the wall of the office and we talked through our route one more time. After a day or so at Union Glacier camp, we would be flown to the edge of the coast on the Ross Ice Shelf at 85°S. This area is designated as the 'coast' because if all the ice melted, we'd be standing on the actual geographic coastline. We would ski across a flat section for about four days and leave the Ross Ice Shelf to follow the Reedy Glacier through the Transantarctic Mountains for about 20 kilometres. From there we'd branch off up the Kansas Glacier and set our own route up to the Stanford Plateau. It would be the first new route to the South Pole by an all-Australian team, and I would be the youngest person ever to have skied a full-route expedition from the coast to the South Pole unsupported and unassisted. There are not many places on the planet's land that someone can travel to and say no other person has ever been there, but we were hoping after this expedition, we could.

Eric showed us where the worst of the sastrugi – the ridges formed by wind that blows around the Pole in an east–west direction at 87° – would likely be, and estimated it would take us three or four days to get through them. We also worked out where we should be on Christmas Day. I'd always dreamed of a white Christmas – but I'd never imagined a Christmas this white!

Considering we'd been delayed on both of the previous two journeys, it was pretty exciting to think we'd be heading off a day before we'd actually planned. We were given a departure time of between 7 am and 7.30 am, so we had to get some sleep and wait for a phone call in the morning. Everything had to be packed up and our hotel bill settled because, once the call came to tell us we were going, we'd only have about 20 minutes before someone arrived to pick us up and take us to the airport. We had to be wearing all of our expedition gear, including our polar boots, to save weight on the plane. I knew I was going to be wearing them for 40 days on the ice – so a few more hours wouldn't hurt. To compensate, the interior of the plane is only warmed to about 12°C so that no one overheats.

It was almost time to leave and I couldn't wait. It would be tough, but I just wanted to get out there. This was the third and final leg of the Hat-Trick. Fulfilling my dream hinged on getting to the South Pole. My mind was plagued by self-doubt, wondering whether I was good enough or strong enough or whether I would fail.

I tried to shake off any negative thoughts. I had to focus, I had to think about the 40 days and 600 kilometres I was about to endure in full-on conditions. I knew the suffering was going to be madness, and I would need to be absolutely, 100 per cent committed to make it all the way to the Pole.

SOUTH POLE VIA KANSAS GLACIER EQUIPMENT LIST

- Sled
- Sled harness
- Polar boots
- Frameless sunglasses with interchangeable lenses
- Goggles
- Climbing ropes, 40 m and 30 m long and 8 mm thick
- Sit harness
- Carabiners (one non-locking keylock and one locking keylock)
- Prusiks, which are loops of 5 mm rope for crevasse rescue
- Skis, bindings, skins
- Ski poles
- Crampons
- Ice screws
- Ice axe
- Warm down-insulated jacket
- Shell jacket and ruff

- Shell pants with braces
- Fleece jacket
- Oversized windproof puffer jacket to pull over all layers
- Thermal tops
- Fleece pants
- Thermal pants
- Ski shorts/skirt
- Underwear
- Fleece-lined polar hat, with ear coverage
- Insulated peak cap, with ear coverage
- Fleece hat for sleeping in tent
- Neoprene face mask
- Neck gaiter or buff
- Polar mittens
- Liner mittens to fit under polar mittens
- Lightweight liner gloves
- Ski gloves
- Vapour barrier socks
- Nylon liner socks
- Thick socks
- Tent with poles, plus two spare
- Tent stakes
- Tent brush, for cleaning snow from the tent floor
- Inflatable mattress
- Camp chair

- Foam seat, for rests
- Sleeping bag, –30°C minimum
- Tent boots
- Snow shovel
- Snow saw, for building snow walls
- Stove with base and shield
- Matches
- Fuel bottle
- Stove fuel, 150 mL per person per day (for 40 days)
- Kettle
- Snow bag
- Food and food boxes (for 40 days)
- Toilet paper
- 1 L thermos flask
- 1 L plastic drink bottle x 2
- Sports bottle
- Bottle parka
- Bowl
- Cup
- Spoon
- Serving spoon
- Pee bottle
- Ice brush
- Compass and harness
- GPS

- Maps and satellite images
- Marker pen
- Medical kit
- Fire blanket
- Personal medications
- Iridium phone and spare phone battery
- Iridium GO and spare GO battery
- Personal Locator Beacon
- Repair kit
- Whistle
- Solar panel
- Storage battery
- Charge cables
- Accessory cord
- Pocket knife/multi-tool
- Camera with spare camera batteries and charger
- AA/AAA batteries
- Watch/alarm
- Passport
- Personal toiletries
- Hand sanitiser
- Sunscreen
- Stuff sacs for packing clothes and food
- Book/Kindle
- Diary and pencil

- Reading glasses
- Ear plugs and eye patches
- Film equipment

My personal equipment list (extras)
- 20 pairs of undies
- Journal
- Letters from friends
- Mishka (the polar bear toy I carried on all my expeditions)
- Australian flag and boxing kangaroo flag
- Small purse full of good luck items (such as the necklace from Villa, the Mars Bar wrapper from Dad's summit day on Everest and blessing band from Lama Geshe on my Everest trek)
- Christmas presents and decorations.

12
THE FIRST 10 DAYS

If there's anything you learn from spending time on an expedition with a bunch of old blokes, it's that you can't be too precious about your privacy. By the end of this trip, I would have spent around 80 days out on the ice with them and the same number of nights sleeping in a tent with my dad. Add to that all the prep days in New Zealand, nights in hotels and hours on planes, and that's a lot of time without the company of people my own age. I realised how much it had changed me when we landed at our starting point on the Reedy Glacier.

We'd taken off in a tiny ski plane bound for our first refuelling stop, about two and a half hours away, where we could take a pee. Because where we were heading was so remote, we were

151

supposed to take a bit of a milk-run route, with two stops along the way to refuel at spots where ALE had left fuel drums on the ice. There was no toilet in the small plane and it was jammed full of our sleds, skis and us. I had been really careful not to drink much water, because the last thing I wanted to have to do was pee into a bottle through my funnel on the plane, less than a metre away from the rest of the team. (Heath and Ming had no issues in this department, as it turned out.) But the plans changed, as they often do on such trips, and after our first refuelling stop, we ended up flying straight through to our drop-off point. We were flying over the Kansas Glacier, which was part of the route we'd be skiing, and were only 10 minutes from landing, when I decided I had to pee – quite badly.

Ming had already told me that he wanted to get off the plane first and film me disembarking, then do a quick interview before we got started. But there was no time for mucking around. Ming and his camera would have to wait. As soon as the door was open, I was on it.

How quickly I had forgotten, though. Apparently there was a 40-knot wind (that's about 75 kilometres an hour) and I was freezing cold already. As I was racing to find a spot, I was tossing up whether I should just drop my pants and go or use the pee funnel. In the end, there was no time for the funnel and I am almost 100 per cent sure the pilots would have got a total eyeful if they'd looked out the window.

We waved goodbye to the plane and as it disappeared into the blue it really hit me that we were now all alone . . . probably the humans most isolated from any other life form on the planet.

The day was already well over halfway through by the time we got ourselves and our sleds sorted out and Ming had all of the footage he needed for the Nat Geo documentary, but we still managed to ski for about four hours all up. The process of making the film always frustrated me to begin with — it was stop-start and I often had a camera in my face at the worst of moments. But I knew that in the end it was really important to be able to share this experience with as many people as possible. I was hoping it would make people care more about these precious and threatened environments. So I sucked it up.

We hadn't been going for long, though, before the sun disappeared behind clouds, the wind picked up even more and the temperatures dropped dangerously — especially for the first day. I definitely felt it physically, especially during the breaks. My legs, back and neck were already aching from the skiing and my bum, thighs and hands had gone numb from the cold. Each expedition began like this, as though we'd gone right back to the beginning. Always in pain. Always trying to establish a rhythm for our days. But that was what the first 10 days on a long expedition are all about — getting used to the place again and establishing good routines. At least for the next few years, this was going to be the last trip I'd have to get used to, even though I certainly plan on future adventures.

We all set our watches back six hours after leaving Union Glacier and it played havoc with our sleep patterns. As the sun shines for 24 hours a day in Antarctica during summer, we could choose any time zone we wanted to operate on. We chose Alaska, as this would put the sun immediately behind us – and our shadows directly in front of us – at midday, making navigation using our shadows and the sun very simple.

On our first morning on the Ross Ice Shelf I woke up at 5.30 am to find Dad getting himself organised and slotting straight back into his polar routine. We'd only got back from Greenland five months previously, so I'd already decided that taking 10 days to find my way back into how things worked out here was far too long. Even physically it felt as though I'd been out on the ice just recently – muscle memory is amazing. It was a little (okay, a lot) harder mentally, though. It took a bit of time to wrap my head around where I was and to block out thoughts of what I might be missing at home: Mum and Kane, my dog, my friends, summer, the beach, good food, a hot shower, my own bed. Of course, 99 per cent of those things remain the same after a while away, but if you can truly block those thoughts out anyway and feel yourself in the moment, you begin to enjoy and appreciate the struggle.

Our early wake-up on day two revealed blue sky and sunshine. It was all the more enjoyable for having hit some bad weather in those few hours on the ice the afternoon before.

On our first full day, we came across the first of what would be many crevasse fields. But it was only a small area, so I needed to trust Eric's expertise in avoiding the worst of them and remember that we'd all been trained in how to get out of them and how to rescue anyone else who fell in. In Greenland, and now on this expedition, I could always tell when Dad recognised crevasse danger from all his years in the mountains, as he would slow down and slot in immediately behind me without saying anything. I knew he was getting himself ready to move quickly if I fell in.

I felt so good for most of the day that I even led the group for a while before lunch. I loved being in the lead, setting footprints where no one had before.

In the next few days, the weather turned foul, and a howling wind woke me at 4.30 on the third morning. The tent was being battered and I could hear the snow against the walls outside. I stuck my head out of the upwind vestibule and saw that my entire sled was buried under a mound of white. I was going to have to dig it out before we went anywhere.

Things didn't improve. The entire day consisted of slogging into the whipping headwind as we took a path towards the mountains. I wore my neoprene face mask (the same material as a wetsuit) and within hours it had grotesque icicles growing where my moist, warm breath had frozen.

We were aiming for the pass between two nunataks (isolated peaks poking out of the ice and snow). It looked close, though up a really steep slope, but the perception was warped. The slope wasn't nearly as steep when we were going up it (good), but it was actually 21 kilometres away (bad).

Even the breaks were incredibly uncomfortable. I'd pull the mask away from my mouth to take a sip of water or eat some of my snacks and, because it was damp from the moisture on my breath, it would freeze against my neck when I put it back on. It was exhausting battling the constant wind, but I needed to get my head in the game. We were still a way off the plateau and I knew from what Eric had told me that the weather would be much worse up there.

My food cravings had already started to kick in. I'm not sure why. Who wouldn't be thrilled at the thought of frozen salami chunks, cheese and two-minute noodles for a month and a half? These are the things I craved at various points of the day in no particular order:

- roast chicken
- a Royale Brothers burger
- Mum's banana bread
- white chocolate and strawberry ice-cream
- a smoked salmon, cream cheese, caper and onion wrap like the one I had on the plane
- the same burger and giant Sprite I had when I finished the North Pole trek
- smashed avocado and goat's cheese on sourdough toast
- eggs and bacon
- Mexican food – anything really, but tacos would be ace
- Vietnamese spicy salad.

Almost everything on that list would have been just around the corner if I was at home, but in Antarctica it was a fantasy.

We set up camp that night between the two nunataks not far off the pass, with the mountains in the distance. We had already covered 47 kilometres since farewelling our pilots and were hoping to reach the Reedy Glacier the next day.

When I called Mum that night she told me everyone back home was excited and very supportive of what I was doing. It was great to hear and it always helped. But I knew that in the end, whether or not I completed this journey was entirely up to me.

I had thought both the North Pole and Greenland were beautiful environments, but Antarctica was something else. I'd seen lots of photos of it, of course, but actually being in the middle of it – feeling the intensity of the cold, being engulfed by the silence and gazing at the mountains – made me feel so alive. And so small.

We cleared the pass first thing in the morning to emerge into an expansive white plain surrounded by mountains. Again, it was deceptive. Once we got close to the ice, it was more of a blue than white colour. We had to negotiate quite a lot of blue ice, which is very slippery, and while this was great for dragging sleds over (they became almost weightless), the skins underneath our skis were useless in terms of trying to create friction so we could plant our feet to move forward. Instead, we would slip around going nowhere. We had to take off our skis and swap them for crampons, which had metal spikes to dig into the blue ice.

The silence out there was beautiful, though. Except for the swish of our ski-pants fabric and the creaking of the heavy sleds against the ice, it was completely still. Maybe sound doesn't travel as far there; perhaps it's muffled by the snow. I guess the noises we hear or don't hear at home are just the background to our lives. But I loved the absence of it.

I was feeling strangely positive about everything. I had quickly established my routine and was facing any difficulties I encountered as calmly and positively as I could. Even when I was struggling physically, I'd tell myself that this was my last expedition and there was no place I'd rather be, despite ongoing issues with the whole toilet situation.

Mont, the Australian company that supplied all my expedition clothing, including the custom pink polar shell I'd worn on all the expeditions, had also created a custom down skirt for me that was a bit like a sleeping bag for my waist. It was an idea I had come up with to attempt to keep the tops of my legs and my bum covered on really cold days, but also when I dropped my pants to go to the toilet. Mont had gone to a lot of trouble to try to make my idea a reality, including various discarded prototypes.

Unfortunately, when the wind is blowing, an extra layer of clothing can be tricky to use effectively. I still managed to get a numb leg and bum when I stopped for a toilet break, and couldn't pull my skirt down properly. The zip came completely undone so I had to remove my mittens to try to fix it. That didn't work. Everyone else had skied off and my hands had become so numb through the inner glove linings that I was losing any feeling in them. I confess I might have teared up a bit at this point, but I managed to get going again.

❄

It didn't take me long to understand that there are good reasons why so few people have skied from the coast to the Pole unsupported and unassisted. It was going to be one long and extremely tough trip. At the end of day five, we made it to the entry to the Kansas Glacier, a steep, moving slab of ice about 60 kilometres long, which no human had ever visited. We were heading directly up it to reach the Stanford Plateau. For the first morning we had to rope up because we were passing through the last part of a crevasse field we'd camped on overnight. It got us off to a late start, and my skirt presented as many problems as it had in the previous days. Our progress was slow since we were roped together for safety as we moved among the crevasses. It was very frustrating and stop-start as the ropes would get caught in our sleds, skis or ski poles.

Once we got to the point where we could separate, I put on some music to find a bit of motivation and lift my pace. It was foggy and windy, but that cleared after lunch. The sun came out and the view of the mountains and landscape was stunning. I led for one of the later sessions, which was one of the coolest things I've ever done. It completely spun me out to think that no one had ever walked on this ground before me. I put on some Jack Johnson and the music, along with the stunning views, set my soul on fire.

The euphoria didn't last long. The next day was rough and I busted my guts to keep going. Even once we'd got through the day, I had to stay out in the cold and wind to do some filming with Ming. I was really looking forward to getting into the tent and warming up a little.

Camp was supposed to be the place where we refuelled and recovered for the next day, but Dad and I were finding it hard to give each other the headspace to relax. It often felt like we were back home in the usual father–daughter patterns of bickering over irrelevant things. It was made worse because we were both exhausted, but there was still so much work to do just to ensure our survival in that harsh polar environment.

Often when I first got into the tent at the end of the day, I was so cold and broken that I had to just sit there in tears on the cold ground, fully clothed, with everything thrown into the tent around me, and not move until I recouped just a little energy. Dad operated differently – he was bustling around at a hundred miles an hour trying to get the nightly tasks done so he could be asleep by 10 pm. I needed time and space to process and think. I would often stay up writing in my journal or listening to music way past the 10 pm 'cut-off'.

I also liked to spend a lot of time on my Instagram posts. Dad seemed to think these could be done in five minutes, but I would often spend up to an hour on each one – choosing the right photo, editing and writing exactly the right words to accompany it. Meanwhile, Dad was beavering away at melting ice and making dinner. This regularly led to arguments about my level of contribution in our tent. And when we were both tired and emotional, we said some things to each other that weren't nice. It was a very unique additional challenge for us – on top of all the usual polar expedition issues, we had to suffer the stress of a strained relationship cooped up in a tent together for around 14 hours every day, while we were both completely destroyed physically and emotionally from the day we'd just endured outside the tent. A lot of the time we just needed to vent and, unfortunately, a lot of the time we were each other's vent.

To make matters worse, that night we tried for ages before we could get Mum on the phone. The line kept dropping out every time she answered. Finally I got a chance to speak to her, and although it helped, I needed more. I wanted to rant to her. I wanted to release. But instead, I had to bottle it all up and just try to get to some sleep. Even now, months later, I can see where the tears made splotches on my journal as I was writing in it that night.

It wasn't going to get any easier. For a start, my Spotify account had logged me out somehow and, because we had no wi-fi, I couldn't log back in. Sticking my headphones in and using music to keep my pace up had helped me through my first two polar journeys, and not having it would make the rest of the days here so much harder. I wasn't sure there was anything I could do to replace the lift listening to music gave me.

The day after, Dad and I had a big argument. We'd finished early, but a combination of sheer exhaustion and a deep conversation about the state of the world with the rest of the team made me wonder why we were even bothering. If people didn't actually care about Earth or the immense danger it was in, they wouldn't bother to make any sort of effective change. I was so far into my head I was in danger of turning inside out. Added to that, the next day we were going to be facing the crux of our journey – the most likely point of failure in this new route to the Pole we were attempting to plot.

It appeared as a huge wall of ice and it had been in our faces for two entire days. At first it just looked like a line on the horizon. It was so intimidating, but I also loved the uncertainty of setting a new route, even though we had no idea what was coming. If we didn't make it over we'd have to find another way to exit the glacier, and we'd already started to look for ways to get around it if it was too massive to get across. The thought of having to backtrack again to look for another route was one of my biggest concerns. Time was so precious.

As it turned out, getting up this enormous rise was a heck of a lot harder than I'd imagined it would be. It was one of the toughest things I'd ever done. Everything else on the other expeditions seemed so much easier by comparison. It was so steep that any time we stopped, even for a few seconds, the sleds would start dragging us backwards down the hill. It was worse for me – I was at the back, and if my sled got away from me there was no way anyone else could help me to stop it. As we kept climbing and climbing, we could see massive crevasses all around us. We had to make sure no one accidentally veered off course.

Both Ming and Heath scratched messages in the snow for me at different points. Ming wrote, 'Ming was here' and

'Go, Jade!', while Heath's message was: 'Jade, you should be really proud of yourself today.'

Finally, we made it to the top, only to find there were another four similar rises – they appeared to be smaller than the first, but they were still large enough to count as major obstacles.

My heart sank. I was exhausted and every part of me screamed in pain. I felt as though I'd used up all my mental resources getting to the top of this rise. To find there were four more was so painful. For a second, my mind hovered around the words 'give up', and actually saying, 'I can't do it.' What would that feel like? I wondered. But even thinking about it made me realise that this quick relief from pain would be nothing compared to the long dark disappointment I would feel in myself.

I put my head down and we trudged forward, everyone lost in their own thoughts, digging deep to find more determination and get through. I broke each rise into a series of single footsteps. One foot after the other, again and again.

We paused briefly at the top of each rise, in recognition that we had knocked off another one, then immediately moved on to the next.

By early afternoon we had made it. We'd opened a new route through the Transantarctic Mountains from the coast to the South Pole. When we'd thought there was just one hill to climb, we'd considered calling it Anzac Rise – instead we 'named' that part of the route Anzac Steps.

After a quick drink and a bite to eat to celebrate, the change in weather conditions reminded us that we were now at the start of the plateau. It was windier and about 10 degrees colder than it had been on the glacier. I put on my jacket, a hat, face mask and goggles, and marched on. In fact, it was much easier to keep going than it had been the day before when the weather was warmer.

We powered through the rest of the day, but I was also worried about what was to come. Arriving at camp, Eric told me, 'This is the plateau. For the next four weeks, this is home.' I wanted to make every moment count, even if deep inside me there was a massive knot of concern about what lay ahead.

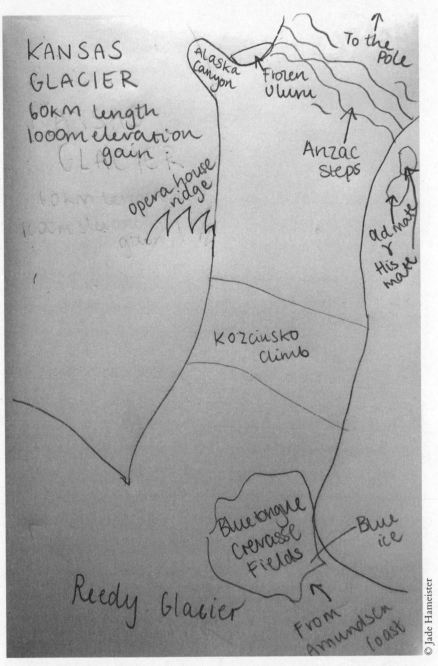

KANSAS
GLACIER
60km length
1000m elevation
gain

Opera house ridge

Alaska Canyon

Frozen Uluru

To the Pole

Anzac Steps

Ad mate & His mate

KOZciusko Climb

Blue tongue Crevasse Fields

Blue ice

Reedy Glacier

From Amundsen coast

A page from my journal – mapping our way through the Kansas Glacier.

SOME COOL FACTS ABOUT...

Antarctica

- Antarctica is the coldest, windiest, highest, driest continent on Earth, and it is also the largest desert in the world.

- At the beginning of winter, as the sea ice extending from the coast begins to freeze, it advances by about 100,000 square kilometres each day until the Antarctic doubles in size.

- The Antarctic ice cap is made up of about 29 million cubic kilometres of ice. That's about 90 per cent of all the world's ice and between 60 and 70 per cent of its fresh water.

- A home freezer runs at about –18°C. The average temperature on Antarctica's high plateau in December and January is about –32°C.

- According to some estimates, if just the West Antarctic Ice Sheet melted, global sea levels would rise by five metres.

- Antarctica's Gamburtsev Mountain Range stretches 1200 kilometres across the continent with peaks rising to a height of about 3000 metres. It is completely buried by ice.

- There are more than 400 subglacial lakes, the largest of which is Lake Vostok, buried about 3500 metres below the ice.

- The existence of Antarctica was unknown until 1820.

- The first person to reach the South Pole was Norwegian explorer Roald Amundsen, who planted the Norwegian flag there on 14 December 1911.

- Robert Falcon Scott, who had already led an expedition to the Antarctic, believed he and his team of four others would be the first to reach the South Pole. When they arrived on 17 January 1912, they found Amundsen's tent, a Norwegian flag and a note. On their return journey, they all perished.

- On 1 December 1959, after a year of secret negotiations, 12 nations signed the Antarctic Treaty, which ensures peaceful research activities are carried out there. Now 48 countries are signatories to the treaty.

- There are about 80 research stations located across the continent, and many of them are occupied year-round.

- Male emperor penguins are the only warm-blooded creatures to stay in the Antarctic during winter, where they sit on a nest containing a single egg. The female penguins take to the sea to fish and come back before the egg hatches.

- The largest land animal in Antarctica is a wingless midge called *Belgica antarctica* that grows up to 6 millimetres long. Most of its life is lived frozen in larval form; its adult life span is no more than a week.

Other than fuel, this was all the gear I carried in my sled to the South Pole (my 40 days of food is in the boxes).

On every expedition, at the end of each day, I would write in my journal. It was a great way to process the hardships and keep a record of my experiences.

The air was so cold in Antarctica that when I threw hot water from my cup into the air it froze instantly.

My neoprene face mask would end up covered with icicles from the moisture of my breath freezing.

Our tent was hammered by the Antarctic winds through the night (and the sun never set – it was 24 hours of daylight) so it was often hard to sleep.

Ming toughing it out to get some footage from behind us in strong polar winds.

Kirby Cone. We were the first humans to see this feature from the ground on the Kansas Glacier, Antarctica.

Approaching the Transantarctic Mountains from the coast.

A slow grind up the headwall at the end of the Kansas Glacier, close to some pretty serious concealed crevasse danger.

© Jade Hameister

This 'parhelion' is a circular rainbow with sun reflections at multiple points.
It happens in Antarctica when wind blows ice crystals high in the sky.

Heath's official role was assistant to the Nat Geo cameraman for Greenland and the South Pole. Unofficially he became my mentor and a true friend.

The challenge of trying to eat noodles with a large plastic spoon while wearing polar mitts with my back to the wind.

White-out on the Antarctic plateau.

Sastrugi — wave-like ridges of hard ice, caused by wind — on the Antarctic plateau.

This was my standard resting position when we had a break at the end of each long session of skiing. Everything ached.

Celebrating Christmas on the way to the South Pole.

Eric, me and Dad at Union Glacier on the way home after reaching the South Pole.

At the South Pole – my Polar Quest finally complete.

Serving up a sandwich for the internet trolls.

13
DREAMING OF A WHITE CHRISTMAS

The routines had been re-established. Each morning we spent almost two hours repeating the same tasks – breakfast, reheating the water for our thermoses (from ice melted the night before), hot drink, brushing our teeth without water, packing up everything inside the tent, 'toilet' stop, taking down camp and packing everything onto the sleds before setting off again for another day of skiing. Our goal was to be on the move by 8 am so that we could finish the day at about 6 pm. With a good pace, we estimated we'd be able to cover sufficient ground during the day to also have a decent amount of time to relax, have dinner and get everything else done in the tent before bedtime at 10 pm. The simple goal was eight hours' sleep, eight hours on the move and eight hours of working time in the tent.

As soon as we hit the Stanford Plateau, the temperature dropped to −30°C overnight, which was about 10°C colder than it had been at the lower elevation. The difficult conditions were a good indication of what we might be facing over the coming weeks, but chances were they'd get worse. At that point, we still had about 450 kilometres to go and 30 days of food remaining, so we were in a good position. But we did need to ensure we were constantly looking after ourselves. To protect yourself from the wind, you have to be wearing lots of layers to ensure no skin is exposed. When we were walking into a headwind, I would always cover my face with a buff (a wrap-around neck scarf), neoprene face mask and goggles. A lot of the time, it could feel quite claustrophobic, especially when my goggles fogged up and I could hardly see where I was going. It was like we almost needed a headset to communicate in the wind (except we didn't have one).

During the breaks, we would sit on our sleds to give our legs a short rest and at lunch we'd use the sleds as both a windbreak and a back rest, while sitting on a piece of foam on the ice. It did protect us a little bit, but out there it was cold even without any wind. Dad would often remove his outer glove so he could press the button on the camera to take a photo of me, and even though his skin was exposed for less than 30 seconds, it always took about half an hour for the feeling to fully return to his fingers.

During that first day up on the plateau, I ended up wearing

an extra down jacket over the top of my polar suit. My chest was bitterly cold the entire time from the moisture in my breath, which froze, then melted again from my body heat and eventually soaked the upper chest of my thermals. When we finally got into our tent at the end of the day the ends of my hair braids were frozen solid to my buff and face mask. All I could do was huddle next to our little camping stove in my freezing clothes, sobbing, unable to feel my fingers and toes, until I thawed out and had enough energy to move again.

It didn't help my mood that Dad kept getting on my case about toilet paper. He told me he only used three double sheets when he did a number two, but didn't seem to understand that I needed to use toilet paper every single time I went to the toilet. I had already begun rationing – I was down to one sheet per pee – but I only had two and a half rolls left. This seemed as though it was going to be a problem with roughly 30 days to go. But Dad had secretly packed a few extra rolls, and he drip-fed them to me each time I ran out, never actually disclosing how many spares he had.

The first few days on the plateau were plain brutal. We were all completely exhausted from the tough climb up the Kansas Glacier, and the conditions – bitingly cold with a strong headwind – were a whole lot worse than I could ever have imagined. We also had to navigate through endless sastrugi. Time and time again, I'd get my ski caught on a ridge in the ice, which would result in a huge jolt and the occasional face plant. At times, I wondered if I was going to be able to go the entire distance, but I had faith that the conditions would get better and the thought enabled me to keep on moving. There was absolutely no way I wanted to quit – not at this point, when we had all come so far and put in so much work.

When we'd stop for a break, it would only take a couple of minutes to lose all the feeling in my fingers. Then my hands were pretty much useless – I couldn't move them. The cold injuries on my thighs were also rubbing against my thermals – something called 'polar thigh'. It was painful while we were skiing, but even worse when we'd finish for the day and climb into the relative warmth of the tent. The frost nip on my butt was aching and was so itchy it made it hard for me to sit still. One night, I couldn't sleep at all. The wind was bashing the canvas of the tent and, for the first time, there was no sun to warm the inside of the tent – it was like being inside a deep freezer. I kept moving and curling up in different positions in an attempt to get warm, but there was just nothing I could do to get comfortable.

Midway through day 12, we were forced to finish early due to horrible conditions, and set up camp. Annoying, but an upside is that eating lunch in the tent is a whole lot easier than trying to get food in your mouth when the bitingly cold wind is whipping around your face and you've got mittens on. Instant noodles and frozen salami also don't taste any better when you're slightly warmer. We did get to eat Pringles, though, and chocolate, and we had Milo too, so that was a big treat.

I started watching one of my all-time favourite movies, *Interstellar*, on Dad's phone, but decided it might be a good idea to take a nap before dinner. Once I shut my eyes I was completely out for about two hours – drool and everything. When I woke up I was disoriented and feeling a bit unwell, but when it was time for dinner I was really hungry again.

That night, I also had a proper chat to Mum. Usually we only have a couple of minutes and it goes something like this:

Mum: Hey, gorge, how's everything?
Me: Good, but tough. How's everything there?
Mum: All good here! How are you coping?
Me: I'm okay. Anything new happening?
Mum: [at this point Mum always found the right story to tell
to lift my mood]
Me: I'll just say good night now before it cuts out again.
Mum: Night, baby. Love you.
Me: Love you, Mum. Night.

The satellite phone would cut out multiple times even during such a short conversation. But that night it didn't once, and I spoke to Mum over the phone for a solid 10 minutes. It was the longest call we'd had since Dad and I had left Punta Arenas.

The lack of sun in the bad weather conditions meant we hadn't been able to charge the satellite modem using our solar panel, so we had to keep phone calls to a minimum. Calling Mum was always a priority for me. Sometimes I got to speak to Kane, but that had only happened twice in those first 12 days and I missed him heaps. I hadn't had a chance to call any of my friends yet either, and I thought about what they would be doing back home at that moment, during our summer holidays. The phone calls with Mum definitely gave me an emotional boost. I couldn't begin to imagine what it must have been like for the early explorers who were cut off from the world completely while on expedition.

That night I fell asleep wondering if we'd wake to −30°C temperatures again, and realising I'd only have to wake up to that kind of cold another 28 times before we reached the South Pole.

The next couple of days were quite kind to us in comparison. Within 10 minutes of starting day 13, we had all stripped off down to our thermals, which helped us make excellent time. We even had a bit of an extended lunch sitting in the sun, before the clouds blew over and it quickly got cold again. Unfortunately, I started feeling like I was getting sick, which was the last thing we needed. All I could think about was my upset stomach, the chilblains on my face and my excruciating polar thigh. In the final hour of the day, though, I decided to take my mind off the pain by practising zoning out. It worked and before I knew it, we were setting up camp while it started to snow.

In an earlier session, Ming and I had skied alongside each other for a while. We'd discussed the fourth dimension, which completely tripped me out, but I loved having conversations like that. Ming is a such a funny guy, even though he doesn't really try to be, and he worked insanely hard throughout the whole trip to make sure it was documented the best it could be. What a legend.

I also spent a bit of time with Heath during a couple of sessions when I was really struggling and feeling quite upset. Like always, he helped me fight the negative feels and push on. He told me that every time you overcome something like that it pushes the best thing that has ever happened to you and the worst further apart. It makes you more able to cope with anything out of the ordinary that lies between these two ends of the spectrum. He told me a story from his experience as a soldier and it gave me a real kick to get a move on. The ability to just get on with it even when everything seems to be against you is so important. While Heath has very strong opinions, we share many of the same views. His motivation was always just what I needed to keep pushing.

For the last session, Dad let me borrow his headphones and music – it was such a good change after having no music for days – and it gave me an immediate boost. By the time I got to camp, I felt as though my attitude had completely turned around.

But for some reason, I couldn't keep it up the next day. It wasn't as though I was feeling sick anymore; I just couldn't get going. At the end of a very slow second session, Eric had a chat to me about needing to do something to pick up the pace and not keep everyone waiting for so long at the breaks. I don't think he meant for it to come across as rude, but for some reason that's how I took it. It gave me the shove I needed, though.

I borrowed Dad's headphones again, put on some hype music and went as hard as I could. Eric and Ming had left the break early because they were getting too cold waiting, but I managed to catch up with both of them. When they next stopped and I was just behind them, Eric told me he was in shock.

Eric and Ming decided to do some interviews at the end of that break. They didn't want me to listen in, so I kept going. I set off at the same pace and it took Eric about 20 minutes to catch up. When he did, he said to Heath, 'Gee, good pace that session, huh?' Heath agreed with him and looked at me, signalling towards his heart. I knew exactly what he meant.

We kept up that pace for most of the day, which made me incredibly sweaty, which is never a good idea because you get cold even faster when you stop for a break. By the final session of the day, I was completely buggered and spent most of it struggling along at the back. When I got into the tent, again I just sat there shivering and sobbing. I wanted to disappear. I couldn't feel my fingers or toes and had trouble holding my head up. Like everyone else, I had icicles hanging off my face. I was in so much pain.

We were still about 20 days from the end, and it wasn't getting any easier. I was struggling and Dad and I were bickering (again). At different times, I had stabbing pains in my stomach and was so cold I couldn't feel anything or use my fingers. At one lunch, I couldn't even hold my spoon and ended up sitting on my mat just staring at the cup of noodles and trying not to cry because I didn't want my tears to freeze. Eric noticed what was happening and came over. He asked me what was wrong, and it was so hard for me to tell him. I didn't have the words. It would take too much effort to say that I felt I had nothing left inside me. No energy. No will to keep moving. No desire even to eat. I didn't want to feel weak or as if I was being supported, especially since all the men were just sucking it up, sitting there eating their lunch as if nothing bothered them. But not eating enough food was also stupid and dangerous. As it's said, a team is only as strong as its weakest member and, at that moment, the weak member was me. I just had to be brave enough to admit it.

Eric spoon-fed me a few mouthfuls of whatever he could get out of my food bag so we could get moving again, as the wind was picking up. He had to help me strap my skis on and put the handles of my ski poles on my wrists, since my hands just wouldn't budge. Even he had to admit this was no place for humans – it really was the coldest, windiest, driest place on Earth. At night, in my sleeping bag, I'd feel so cold I could barely hang on to a pencil (the ink in pens freezes in the cold) to write in my diary. Despite the struggle, we were still managing to cover 17 or 18 kilometres each day, which was enough to keep my head high.

It was almost 25 December and I was super excited to have my first white Christmas in Antarctica, except it didn't feel like Christmas at all. The thought of what would've been going on at home and not being able to spend the day with family and friends by the beach was getting me down. The day before Christmas Eve in Antarctica it was Christmas Eve at home (following different time zones), and we were trapped in our tents during a blizzard. We'd had to set up camp early the day before as conditions had worsened. It was so bad we had to stack the sleds on top of one another as a windbreak, so we could get the tents up as swiftly as possible. It was dark, as the snow and clouds completely blocked out the sun, making it hard to see the features of the ground. It wasn't easy, and we were forced to use ice screws to hold the tent down in the hard ice. Even though the ice was rock solid, Dad still had to try to shovel some around the edges of the tent to add some weight and block the wind from tunnelling underneath. Eric had already broken one shovel doing the same thing, so we had to be really careful not to make the same mistake twice, since we only had one shovel left, which we were now all sharing.

All night, the blizzard thumped against the side of the tent. The walls of the tent shook, and because the sun had been hidden when we set up camp, both of our air mattresses were parked on large clumps of ice. Normally I'm the lightest sleeper ever, but I somehow managed to sleep right through the noise until Eric woke us up at 6 am. He told us to stay where we were because we were going to have to keep inside the tents for the day. Luckily, we'd been making some great time, even over the difficult fields of sastrugi. It was a good chance to get some rest, while we waited out the storm. I crashed again until 9 am, when Dad woke me up for breakfast. For the rest of the day, we slept, ate, watched movies, slept and ate.

Later, when we called Mum, she read out some of the comments I'd been receiving on my Instagram posts. It really meant a lot to me that so many people were following the journey and backing the whole team.

It is possible to keep moving during a blizzard – we had the gear, clothes and high-energy food to keep us going – but it gets really dangerous when you have to stop to eat or hydrate. You lose heat a lot quicker than normal. It's also very difficult to navigate in a blizzard. Any features in the landscape were invisible to the eye.

Thankfully, Christmas Eve in Antarctica brought some better weather. We were still moving through sastrugi zones, but from the old map we had of this unexplored area, it seemed as though there would only be another five or six days of it. That's the big difference between the route we were taking and the traditional route most teams choose to take. In total, we'd spend about 10 days dealing with the ups and downs of the sastrugi and all the face plants and snapped ski poles that they brought with them (Dad had already broken one of his). The ice was very hard – almost like glass in places – so, in theory, you should be able to cruise across the top of it. But the reality was different.

By now we'd covered around 100 kilometres of sastrugi and had about the same distance still to go before finding a flatter surface. It was like skiing on a choppy, frothy ocean that had been frozen in time – impossible to find any rhythm skiing across it. You're constantly being jerked backwards when your sled hits a hard ridge or you fall over when the tips of your skis hit a solid bit of ice that you can't kick through. It was really hard work, and you can't mentally switch off and take yourself somewhere else like you can when you're skiing across a flat surface. You have to concentrate on every step. Of course, we knew there would be these challenges when we decided to take on this new route, but knowing and doing are so different.

At one point during the day, Ming had taken his skis off to do some filming with me. The others had gone off in front of us, and once we'd finished filming I'd just dropped my pants to do a wee when I heard a yell. I turned around to see Ming, about 50 metres away, chest-deep in a crevasse and clinging to its edge. I completely freaked out – we must be in a crevasse field – and, with my pants still down, I unclipped from my sled and started running towards him, yelling at the others who were too far away to hear. Within a few seconds, however, he'd managed to haul himself out, rolled over on the flat ground and gave me the thumbs-up. Thank gosh. Once I'd pulled my pants up again and started moving, I skied past the crevasse on my own and looked down where it followed into the abyss. Thin walls of rough, rigid blue ice shards led deep down to nothing but black. It seemed bottomless and I felt a shiver up my spine. I was staring into my nightmare. Ming had had a very lucky escape and we were able to laugh about it later on.

Towards the end of the day, we hit another big hill of ice. It was a tough ascent, but luckily for us, we weren't trying to navigate through a maze of sastrugi and crevasses anymore. The highlight of the day, though, was reaching the halfway mark to the Pole. Halfway made the whole way seem possible.

That night, in the tent, I opened a Christmas card from Zoe, who has been one of my best friends forever. There was a little block of chocolate inside – heaven – but there was also a photo of a roast Christmas turkey. What sort of person sends you a photograph of delicious food when you're living off two-minute noodles and dehydrated beef and peas?! It was so cruel, but it made us laugh.

I don't think there's a stranger place to wake up on Christmas morning than a tent in the middle of Antarctica. Ming had snuck into the tent before I'd even opened my eyes to make sure he got the morning on film. The night before, we'd put up some tinsel and a little snowman key chain as decoration, so it felt slightly festive. Dad had a little present for me, as well as some cards from home. He handed them over and we opened them up while we were still wrapped inside our sleeping bags.

Dad handed me a tiny present and I unwrapped it to find a blue Tiffany box inside. Mum and Dad had bought me a beautiful bracelet – where it joined they'd chosen a design that they thought represented the North Pole and the South Pole. It was really special, and Dad told me it was one of the only presents that he'd been involved in buying (this was a big statement as usually Mum does that job very well).

Then I got a nosebleed, which was such a great way to begin the day, as toilet paper was almost as valuable as gold.

We had an extra 20 minutes on top of our normal morning time this morning, so we soon put the stove on and got on with breakfast and preparing for the day. Despite being Christmas Day, we needed to cover enough ground so we didn't get behind. Moving would also be a good way to take my mind off the Christmas I was missing out on at home.

Eric had his Santa hat on while we were packing up our sleds, but that was about as much humour as he had for us that morning. He believed the day ahead of us was going to be really tough and we should be happy with even getting out of the tents. The wind had blown right up again overnight, and it felt colder than any other day so far. Aside from the howling wind, it was overcast, so we weren't going to get any heat from the sun. The landscape hadn't changed really — we could still see plenty of sastrugi ahead.

The first four hours were spent walking into the strongest winds we'd had the whole trip. It also began snowing, so my dreams of a white Christmas were coming true, except it was a nightmare. The wind wasn't just making things extremely cold — it was also making it hard to communicate, making us all a bit tense and anxious. Taking a decent break wasn't really an option either, since stopping for too long meant you'd end up so cold you'd start to lose all the feeling in your extremities.

The conditions were awful, but we'd made a commitment to ski as far as we could and we were going to stick with it for as long as we could. Eric was being really cautious in these dangerous conditions. No one was allowed to stand around for too long because he was worried we'd end up either frostbitten or hypothermic. We'd also come across a few crevasses the day before, but they are really hard to see when the snow is being pushed across the surface of the ice in heavy drift and there's little to no visibility. When the snow drift is that strong it's almost like you're skiing into a rushing white river as the snow howls past your legs like an endless stream of raging ghosts.

Eric had packed a small shelter (a human-sized bag made of tent-like material to block the wind) in his sled and at lunchtime he got it out for the first time to see if it would provide some protection during our lunch break. Dad and I pulled it over and around ourselves. There's nothing special about having lunch in what is basically an oversized rubbish bag. And we hadn't packed anything special either, so Christmas lunch was the same as every other day – noodles with crackers, some butter and a chunk of frozen salami. The snow drift found a way inside the shelter and whipped around, so within minutes we were caked in a dusting of snow. It was a miserable failed experiment.

That night we had a little get-together in the other tent and celebrated Christmas Antarctica-style. I felt it had been the toughest day yet, but to make up for it, we all shared some chocolate, Tim Tams and Milo that Eric had been hiding, while Dad played some Frank Sinatra Christmas carols over his Bluetooth speaker.

Later we called Mum and Kane from our tent. The first time we tried to get through to them it rang out, but Kane finally answered.

For me, Christmas is about spending time with family and friends. I was with Dad, of course, but I also felt the rest of our team had become part of my extended family. We were sharing something that hardly anyone else would ever understand. Eric had spent about 10 Christmases away from home in Antarctica guiding different expeditions, and I'm pretty sure it wasn't easy for him to be gone either, especially because he had kids my age back home. Like Dad and me, he was missing his family a lot. He told us it would probably be his last Christmas in the Antarctic.

There were no hangovers or sore tummies from too much dehydrated turkey the next morning. What did arrive, though, was the weather forecast – and it wasn't good. The winds were predicted to pick up even more over the next five to six days and it made my stomach churn with anxiety. Early on Boxing Day, it didn't seem to be too bad, but that was possibly because the conditions on Christmas Day had been so terrible. Since it was going to get a lot worse in the next week or so, we really needed to step up the pace and get some kilometres under our belt just in case we had to stop again because of high winds. Dad told me he was once trapped in a single-person tent for 11 days at high camp on Denali, the highest mountain in North America, and had run out of food (and toilet paper!). That can basically kill an expedition. We needed to take these weather windows seriously and gain as much distance as we could.

By day 22, we had 18 days' worth of food and fuel left and 267 kilometres to go to get to the Pole. At that point, it had all become about maths and battling the elements. We needed to cover very close to 15 kilometres every day for the next 18 days or so, or we were going to run out of provisions. But because the bad weather was on its way, I felt as though we should be aiming to do much more than that, especially on days when it was at least partially clear.

For four days in a row, we'd pushed to cover 17 kilometres, and it was our last day of trying to hit that distance. For the next 10 days, we were going to try to bump that up to 20 kilometres a day to reach the South Pole on 10 January as planned. That gave us four days' leeway in case of any injuries or more bad weather. The terrain ahead looked a lot like what we'd been facing for the last week. The sky was blue at least, but, no surprise . . . it remained windy.

Dad had given me something to look forward to in the evening. With the sun shining and good solar power to our satellite modem, he suggested I make some late Christmas calls to my best friends, whom I hadn't been able to speak to at all since we'd started the trip almost a month ago. When I called, Zoe spent the whole time running around trying to find better service in the small town she was staying in for the holidays. Mia was enjoying her summer holiday with another of my close friends, Paris, so she put the phone on speaker. It was so hard to get my head around the fact that my friends were at the beach and I was about as far away from one as was possible.

When I'm at home, my friends and I don't talk about my polar expeditions. Our life together is in Melbourne. They see some of the media, but other than that, we don't spend a lot of time on it. I really enjoy not talking about it with them and being able to relate in other ways. It's hard to conjure up the person who lugged a 100-kilogram sled across Antarctica and sobbed with pain at the end of long tough days. Having said that, the letters Zoe and Mia wrote for me during the trips for motivation were incredibly special, and I always tried to open them when I was at a low point and needed a bit of loving.

In terms of the cold and the wind, the conditions were so much worse than those at the North Pole. Both that and crossing Greenland were great experiences and taught me how to struggle and deal with pain, but this had been by far the toughest leg of the Polar Hat-Trick.

And we still had a long way to go.

SOME COOL FACTS ABOUT...

Saving the Planet

These are some classic but simple things you can do every day to help protect the planet. If we all contributed, there'd be a huge reduction in pollution and wasted resources.

- Turn off the lights every time you leave a room, and switch any appliances with standby power off completely.

- Open windows and close blinds to cool your house rather than turning on air-conditioning. When it's cold, put on woolly socks, grab a blanket or pull on a cardigan rather than turning on the heating.

- Take public transport, ride your bike, consider car pooling and try to combine lots of errands into one trip to cut down how much your family uses its vehicles.

- Only use the washing machine or dishwasher when there's a full load. Always hang your clothes on the line rather than using a dryer.

- Either plant vegetables to grow your own food or fill your garden with native plants, which require far less water than introduced species and attract insects and birds.

- Opt for paperless billing and emailed bank statements wherever you can.

- Buy a good reusable water bottle and coffee cup and use them all the time.

- Try to banish all single-use items – whether they're plastic takeaway containers, plastic straws or disposable razors – from your home.

- Fix things rather than throwing them out, and donate any clothes or things you don't use to charity.

- Ensure you understand if your recycling is functioning properly.

- Reduce food waste by having a menu plan and sticking to it each week, cooking with leftovers and freezing food before it goes off.

- Eat less processed food.

- Take shorter showers.

- Always carry reusable shopping bags with you, so you're never caught out having to use plastic ones at the supermarket. Invest in some reusable produce bags, too.

14
WELCOME TO 2018

I am not a morning person. You have probably gathered that by now.

The time it took for me to properly wake up and get ready for each day on the ice may have driven Dad a bit crazy. But you'd think that after 22 days, plus expeditions to the North Pole and across Greenland, he may have come to terms with it.

I'd come to realise that nothing out there was going to be easy, and the days after Christmas didn't prove me wrong. It started out badly enough. I was frozen through and sluggish. Energy seemed to have completely left my body. We had hit the uphill ascent over the shoulder of the Titan Dome, but I tried to tell myself we were on the downhill stretch as far as the whole journey was concerned.

Eric said he thought I probably wasn't managing to get enough calories into my body, which was inevitably slowing me down. Somehow, though, I ate quite a lot of food at lunch that day. I'd managed to stay quite warm, which helped a lot. I was able to hang on to my spoon properly, so I could get my noodles to my mouth, and now I was feeling great about everything. I seemed to be up and down, down and up, the emotional extremes mirroring the environment. No one else seemed to be experiencing such intense mood swings, but I was facing many of these mental and physical challenges for the first time, while many of the others had years of adventuring under their belts.

At least now I had mastered the art of losing myself in the motion of skiing. You have so much time to yourself and with your own thoughts that if you let your brain get started you begin to overthink absolutely everything – something I was already guilty of. Zoning out is by far the better option. The longer I spent skiing the better I got at taking myself to another place, which made the time go so much faster.

One thing I did out there a lot that I never do at home was checking in with myself: how I was feeling, what I needed to tell myself to keep my body moving, how I could best look after myself physically and emotionally. It's so easy nowadays to get sucked into distractions like our phones and miss what is really going on around us and in our minds. It was a really good opportunity for me to learn something about myself.

In the time I spent thinking, what amazed me most was that the part of Antarctica we were skiing across was very similar to where the early explorers, like Amundsen and Scott, had travelled more than a hundred years ago. They would have been battling the same cold and the same wind. They would have seen the same magical formations in the snow and the shimmering halos around the sun. The high-tech fabrics and gear we have access to today do make it a little more comfortable, though. And, of course, if something went wrong for us, as tricky as it may have been for a rescue operation to be mounted, it could happen. Back then they would have just had to deal with it themselves.

We'd hit another milestone recently, which was great mentally and gave everyone in the group more motivation to keep skiing: we'd finally broken through the notoriously difficult band between 87° and 88°S. Between those two degrees there is a circumpolar wind travelling from east to west that creates the sastrugi that had been incredibly painful to navigate. Now, the terrain was beginning to flatten out, which meant we'd be able to pick up the pace and cover more distance.

The next big milestone, and we expected to hit it very soon, was reaching the point where we were 200 kilometres from the South Pole. We were still climbing, though, and were at an elevation of about 2950 metres above sea level – actually higher than the South Pole itself. We could definitely feel the thinner air's effect on our breathing and we were all struggling more than usual. However, we got a real fright when Eric started to suffer some of the real symptoms of altitude sickness. It's a weird condition that can strike quickly – whether or not you are fit has little to do with whether you'll suffer or not. At first, we didn't even realise what was happening to Eric. I noticed him stopping and leaning forward with his chest over his ski poles, and I thought maybe his back was giving him some grief so he was just taking a quick break. But then he sat down on his sled, which he rarely did, even during breaks. He told me his heart had started to flutter, then he got heartburn and his body began to feel incredibly heavy. He'd had altitude sickness before and almost had to be evacuated from the plateau in 2013 when his lungs began filling up with fluid. Thankfully, he knew how to deal with it and took some medication that seemed to help a lot. Heath took the lead for a while so that Eric could take it a little easier. We still managed to cover 19 kilometres on another tough day.

A couple of days later, having battled through more white-outs and the extreme cold, it was New Year's Eve in the Antarctic. Normally, I'd have a pretty quiet day at home then go out with my friends in the evening. This year was very different. For a start, it was one of the toughest days I'd had. I couldn't get myself moving in the first two sessions of the day and slowed down the whole group. I suspect that I was feeling the altitude a little bit too, because I was having trouble breathing and had a fairly intense headache. I was still having issues with the chill on my chest, too. I had completely forgotten what it felt like to be warm. There was no sympathy for me, though. Dad wanted to know what the matter was, and I was asked to decide whether I really wanted to finish this or not, because if we continued at the pace I'd been moving that morning, we would not make it to the Pole without running out of food and fuel. But giving up hadn't even crossed my mind. We were nine days from the finish, and I was going to make it no matter what. Plus, I knew I was doing the best I could surrounded by four grown men who were more than double my age. I knew I had to do something about the negative self-talk that was invading my head whenever I was feeling a bit off, otherwise it was going to make the last few days hell when I should've been making the most out of being in this incredible landscape, even if it was hard to love sometimes.

Heath decided to hang back with me and let the others ski ahead. He kept telling me that the best way to warm up was to get moving, to put one foot in front of the other. But in that moment, I was in Struggle Town. It was −50°C with wind chill and I don't think I'd ever been colder. I was genuinely worried that my hands were so cold I was going to lose fingers. Tears filled my eyes and for about 30 minutes I struggled to keep going. But, as soon as I started to speed up and push harder, I forgot about the pain through warming up. I became a completely different person – one who was much nicer to herself and the people around her.

I didn't get to speak to Mum that night. I wanted her to have a chance to chat to all my friends, so she could tell me in full the next day what they'd been up to for New Year's Eve the night before. I really wanted to know; I didn't want to miss out on anything. It didn't at all feel like the start of a new year to me, and my friends, family and the Australian summer seemed a long way off yet.

One annual family tradition Dad and I did continue was setting our goals for the coming year. It's something he has always done and he had encouraged Kane and me to do it ourselves from quite an early age. We set goals under a range of different categories – everything from health and fitness, to school. We normally sit down and go through them with Dad when we've had a go ourselves, and also check back through the ones we'd made the previous year to see how we'd done. For me, 2018 was going to be about focusing on school and getting back on track, recovering and taking some time to figure out what was next in terms of adventure, spreading my messages about female empowerment and climate change, and meeting new people and learning from them. My goals were definitely smaller in some ways than they had been for a few years. This was the first time in ages I didn't have a huge adventure goal and an expedition to work towards.

Talk about a big night New Year's Eve. To go crazy, we had some extra Pringles plus a freeze-dried dessert. Mine was a cinnamon rice pudding and it looked as though someone had vomited in my bowl, but it tasted pretty good. We were all asleep by 10 pm.

My first task for 2018 was to lead the group during the first session of the day. Part way through the Greenland crossing the year before, when I was out the front leading the group, Heath had taught me how to navigate using the sun along with a compass.

That morning, I was able to use the sun. For that time of day, I had to position myself at a 45-degree angle to my shadow, pick a distinctive point in the distance, like a piece of sastrugi, and ski towards it.

Instead of our recent strategy of skiing for 2.5 kilometres to make each break, we decided to push on for an extra 100 metres. It doesn't sound like a lot, but it meant we finished the days earlier, which was always a good thing. However, I was to go at my own pace, since the first session was mine.

It was tough going . . . not unusual. We were still moving directly into a strong, icy headwind, and the snow was particularly sticky, which made it harder to drag the sleds. But we managed to ski more than 17 kilometres during the day, which means the shocking conditions weren't holding us back too much. We were getting so close to the end of the journey, I could feel it.

That night, something incredibly odd happened. We were in the tent, having dinner, when we heard this deep, loud rumble coming towards us. Then there was a thump as the snow we were camped on dropped a couple of centimetres beneath and around us, then the rumble disappeared into the distance. I had no idea what was going on, but Eric soon came to tell us that we'd just experienced a snow quake. It's basically the snow collapsing into an air pocket below it, triggered by the wind and melting ice, but it moves along at a couple of hundred metres per second. Eric said it was the biggest and loudest he had ever experienced, but it wasn't anything to worry about despite me having a mini heart attack!

Our last milestone was during the next day, when we crossed the final degree of latitude (89°S) on our way to 90°S. Each degree is separated by 112 kilometres, so we were almost there. We might now come across some other teams, most of which skiied the last degree, but it would have been pretty easy to tell them apart from us. We'd been out here for 30 whole days now without a shower and wearing the same clothes – so we'd be the scrawny, shattered, stinky ones.

Our last few days were like many of the 30 before them. The sun was shining but the conditions continued to test us. We were covering good ground, but some nights I'd crawl into the vestibule of the tent and just sit on my knees shaking with the cold, almost unable to hold my head upright. I was really looking forward to sleeping in my own warm bed when I got home, with a proper pillow.

The only new part of our routine for this last week was the requirement to poo into a bag and carry it with us to the Pole. It's compulsory for anyone within the final degree of the South Pole to do this. If carrying your own waste around in a bag sounds bad to you, get this: to save on weight in the sled, Eric had decided to bring only enough bags for every second day of this last leg, so we had to use each bag twice. If he had told me that when we were packing the sleds, I'm pretty sure I would have volunteered to carry the extra few bags in my sled to save us all the indignity.

Day 36 was our final full day out on the ice. The weather must have known this was a special day for us because when I crawled out of the tent, the sun was shining, the sky was blue, there was little wind for the first time I could remember and it was only about −30°C.

We climbed a small rise in the morning and after the second session, in the distance, we could see a tiny black line on the horizon: the Amundsen–Scott South Pole Station. I didn't really believe that's what it was until I got a little closer and the other guys confirmed it. Directly ahead of me was the end of three crazy years. There had been times in the past few years when I'd really wondered if I would ever get to this point. Eric had said he'd never encountered such brutal conditions in Antarctica in all his 25 years guiding polar expeditions. Now, we were so close I could start picking out different features. Later in the day we even saw a Russian military plane land and take off again.

That night, we had to camp at a waypoint nine kilometres from the South Pole. It's really just a sign that says POLE TURN 1 on the ice road with a few coloured flags attached to it. Teams coming in from this side of the station (most come from the opposite side) have to wait for clearance to enter towards the Pole, just in case there are any aircraft coming in. We'd been asked to follow the road to the Pole, but we didn't want to jeopardise the unsupported status of our expedition. We'd managed to go the whole journey without outside assistance and didn't want to travel even for a short distance on a road made by another vehicle, so we skied off to one side of it.

It felt so weird to put up the tents, turn on the stoves, heat the water and get dinner ready for the last time. This chapter of my life was about to end and it was only just now really sinking in.

❄

Eric called the final day of the expedition 'Pole Day'. We'd decided to wake up early and get going. By the time we got out of the tents I was feeling all sorts of emotions: chuffed to be so close to achieving such a huge goal, excited to think we'd be heading home in the next few days, but also sad; I knew I'd miss this cold, windy place that had caused me so much pain and suffering but had really opened my eyes to its exquisite beauty. Antarctica was now a part of me.

I wasn't convinced that this was to be my last-ever day in a polar environment, though. Dad reckoned he'd seen enough snow and ice to last a lifetime, and Eric was fairly convinced that, after 25 years of guiding, this would be his last long-distance trip in the polar regions. In that time, he'd completed four coast-to-Pole journeys (including ours), which is definitely not something that many people can claim.

Dad and I tied a boxing kangaroo flag to the back of my sled and off we went, skiing beside the road for the final kilometres. We'd decided to tackle them in four shorter sessions and I was out the front for most of the way. I was so keen to get there. In the distance, we saw someone on a skidoo going about their business at the station, which was an incredibly weird sight after seeing no other sign of life for a month. The smell of fumes from the station was also obvious and so strong for us after only breathing in pure air for weeks.

We tried to stick together, but it was difficult with Ming directing me as he tried to capture everything he wanted for the film. We could see the Pole but our progress was so stop-start that the moment was kind of lost. To begin with, reaching the Pole was slightly underwhelming. I had to stand beneath the flags of all the countries that are signatories to the Antarctic Treaty and wait for Ming to frame everything just right. I was told I had to ski in around the flags and cut in towards the Pole next to the Australian flag rather than just going for it.

Once I got the all clear, I could ski right up to it and touch the glass ball on top of a barber's pole marking the Geographic South Pole. It was surreal, like I wasn't even really there. Like I was watching from above and unsure what to do next. It went incredibly quickly. I started to tear up – emotions were high, but it was all tempered by having to follow directions from Ming. Not even 30 seconds after I'd first reached the Pole, I had to go back to the flags and do it all again to make sure we got the shot Ming was after. It was hard to process what was happening – there was so much going through my head. We had made it. But knowing that almost made me kind of numb as well, especially having to record everything on camera. It probably made me feel a little removed from the enormity of what was happening and where I was. Maybe that would come later, when I had a chance to really think about the journey in my own time.

Dad made a little speech about how proud the family was and how he knew I would be capable of dealing with anything life threw at me (he gave me a letter from Mum that I was to save until later) and we took some photographs with the family's Australian flag, which we carry with us on every adventure. Then it was time to head to ALE's camp. It was over.

Among a number of unexpected records, I had achieved my original simple goal – to complete the Polar Hat-Trick.

I'd been aware of almost none of the records when we'd begun planning these expeditions three years ago, but it was an extraordinary feeling to make history.

Now for a hot meal at camp.

15
THE END OF THIS CHAPTER

To my darling baby girl. As I sit here writing this letter to you, you are upstairs tucked up in a warm safe bed. As you read this you will be in one of the coldest, most extreme parts of the planet, a long way from your mama. I am feeling loads of emotions today, as I write, and a load more on the day you are reading this. To let your little girl wander off into the big world is extremely daunting for a mum. My natural instinct is to wrap you up from anything that may harm you or hurt you, however I know deep down that this would be harmful for you. You were born a fighter; you fought to survive when you first entered this world, and now you are fighting to make your mark. I am extremely proud of the young woman you are today. Your journey into adulthood is just beginning and what a way to start. This chapter of your life will be a drawing point for so many more challenges you face. I'm really looking forward to seeing you grow further and enjoying all life has to offer you. Enjoy and remember every last part of this chapter and hold it close to you forever. I couldn't be prouder and happier for you. I burst with pride. Look forward to a big squeeze soon.

Love you the most,

Mum xxx

This was the letter Dad handed to me when we arrived at the South Pole. It was so special, and I wished Mum was there with me so I could give her a big hug.

It was so hard to believe we'd made it, and it still is, but little reminders like this were helping it all sink in. And, as eager as I was to get home and see everyone, I was also glad we had a few days left in this unique environment to enjoy, since we had to wait for one of the last-degree teams to arrive to share our plane back to Union Glacier. When I was out on the ice and the conditions were doing their best to blow us off the plateau, all I could think about was getting home. But the thrill of adventure is addictive. Even with the thought of family, friends, hot showers and good food just days away, there was part of me that never wanted to leave.

The weather stayed clear and the other team (last degree only) arrived on time, so we flew from the Pole back to Union Glacier on schedule. The plane was so cool – built in 1942 and the same type that was used during World War II. I took my face mask and goggles off for a few minutes before we boarded, just so that I could get a few photos in Antarctica with my face actually visible. I was very quickly reminded why we had never gone bare-faced out there. My nose would have been nipped by the frost in no time and the glare from the sun on the snow meant I could barely keep my eyes open. Despite the amazing views below me, within a few minutes of the plane taking off I had fallen asleep.

The flight to Union Glacier Camp was about three and a half hours and we were due to spend two nights there before flying back to Punta Arenas.

It was so good to be able to spend time with other people, after almost six weeks with the same four grotty men. The other much-appreciated aspect of having finished the expedition was proper food. I'd put on about 6.5 kilograms before the trip here, and when I weighed myself at the camp I'd lost seven kilos. Not surprisingly, after bringing my tastebuds back to life with some French onion soup, homemade chocolate chip cookies and fresh fruit, I couldn't stop eating. Eating a proper dinner was amazing, particularly since dessert was fruit pie and cream.

We met another team of adventurers at the camp: Leo Houlding, Jean Burgun and Mark Sedon, who had just completed their 'Spectre' Expedition. They'd been out on the ice for almost two months and, with the assistance of kites, had travelled about 2000 kilometres. They'd also ascended a large unclimbed rock face in the Gothic Mountains, one of the most remote ranges in the world. It was amazing to trade stories with them and compare journeys. Leo had previously featured in the documentary *The Wildest Dream*, which tracks the ascent of Everest by explorer George Mallory, who died on the North-east Ridge in 1924. Leo also had a baby daughter, so was quite interested in my story.

The trip that the trio had just completed was absolutely extraordinary. Some of the footage they showed us from their expedition was incredible, and although I'm not a big fan of rock climbing, it really got me thinking about things I might like to do in the future.

Almost immediately after returning home from Antarctica, I had to go back to school to start year 11 – or, as all parents and teachers will tell you, the first of two of the most important years of your life. It's not that I don't like school, but after everything I'd been through it was (and still is) hard to get motivated and stay focused, particularly when there is so much else going on around me. Turning up to classes five days a week is okay – but finding the time and motivation to do homework and extra study has been hard. But I realised I needed to shift my focus. For the past three years, my focus has been on completing the Polar Hat-Trick; now it has to be on finishing school and doing as well as I can.

There are so many other things that I'd rather be doing, though, so refocusing on school hasn't been easy. I want to try to make a difference in the areas I care about. I want to keep exploring and pushing boundaries. While my school and my teachers have been incredibly supportive, the school system just doesn't allow the flexibility I need, so I feel a bit caged.

There's one question I keep hearing now: What's next? And it's a really tricky question because I don't know the answer, but feel like I should.

There is only so much I can describe to people about my experiences, but I think a deeper understanding of the environment we were in and how I was feeling will come out of the Nat Geo documentary and this book – which is why they are now so important to me. This book, especially, conveys so much more of the story behind the scenes and I hope that, in sharing my experiences, I will inspire people to care about the incredible planet we call home, live their dreams and make a difference.

For me, it seems hard to grasp that, in the short term at least, there are no new adventures on the horizon. Having completed something that has involved so much time and hard work has definitely left me in a bit of a lull since being home. I've had plenty of things to look forward to, but not having something big to work towards right now has left a hole. There are times when all I want to do is return to the snow because, as hard as it is, it is a really simple way of being and far from any other forms of existence. You have a single goal, and that's to survive and get through another day. All of life's excesses are stripped away. You need food, water, warmth and the will to keep pushing, not much else.

There's a phenomenon I have recently become aware of called 'the overview effect'. I didn't know if what I was feeling was common, but I discovered that astronauts often feel it, too. When they're in space looking back at Earth and at the stars they realise just how small we really are. 'A cognitive shift in awareness' is how Wikipedia describes it. I have the exact same feeling after living in such remote and hostile locations with only a few other people within thousands of kilometres around me. It has completely changed the way I think about the universe and our place in it. It makes me think about everything I've done in the past, what I want to achieve in the future and whether it means very much at all. Realising that we and our planet are just a tiny speck in an infinite universe gives you a completely different perspective on life.

I don't want to be known as a polar explorer or polar adventurer. This has been just a chapter in my life that is now complete and I am ready to move on to the next.

As I made my way along this journey, there are three things that became really important to me. And they became clearer, the further along the journey I got. The first was empowering young women to shift their focus from how they appear to the possibilities of what they can do. The second was to inspire young people to choose bravery over perfection. And finally, to raise awareness of climate change and the effect it's having on our planet.

I also have a growing interest in entrepreneurship, and space travel and exploration. Elon Musk is a big idol of mine. Earth is currently our only known habitable planet, and I believe we must try to do our *absolute* best to protect it. But I also believe there is so much potential beyond Earth, in the largely unexplored universe, for other planets to sustain life. With the constant advances in technology, and the entrepreneurial passion of so many powerful human beings, I am positive we can work together to design a future in the stars.

I'm excited to see where the next chapter of living takes me.

Thank you for your support on my journey so far. x

ACKNOWLEDGEMENTS

I'm especially grateful to the following people for their incredible support of my polar dream:

Dad for believing in my dream, dedicating so much of his time to making it a reality and for all the unique memories we've shared as father–daughter.

Mum for all of her love and support and for suffering the loneliness of having Dad and me away from home for such a long time pursuing my dream.

My brother Kane for his unconditional friendship, love and support, for all the laughs and more to come.

My extended family, especially my grandparents Grandy and Papa, my Auntie Karen who is my biggest supporter,

Uncle Johnny and Auntie Emma for everything they've done for me.

All my friends for their support, especially my best friends, Zoe and Mia, for the letters they wrote to keep me motivated throughout all three expeditions, and Cooper and Will for their love and support back home.

Eric Philips and his company, Icetrek, for organising the logistics for each expedition and being a very professional, knowledgeable and great guide.

Petter Nyquist for being the first cameraman I have ever dealt with (and being so supportive and patient).

Heath Jamieson for being my first true mentor, teaching me about myself, how to be a better human and for becoming such a great friend along the way.

Ming D'Arcy for being such a dedicated cameraman and for encouraging chats about the fourth dimension.

Frederique Olivier for being camerawoman on the Greenland expedition.

Vilborg Arna Gissurardóttir (Villa) for being such a strong female role model and inspiring me to embark on my own polar journeys.

The team at the documentary production company, WTFN, especially Daryl Talbot, Steve Oemecke, Wes Crook and Olwyn Jones. A special mention to Wayne Dyer, the Producer of both Nat Geo documentaries for his passion and dedication to his craft and becoming an extended member of our family.

Everyone at National Geographic Channel and National Geographic Society, especially Jules Oldroyd, Global Head of Programming, for making the decision to support my expeditions and everything else she did to welcome me into the Nat Geo family, including facilitating my attendance at two Explorers Symposiums in Washington. Also, the Australian team at Nat Geo and Fox, especially Jerry Butterfield.

The team at the Australian Geographic Society for their support and sponsorship, especially Chrissie Goldrick and Rebecca Cotton.

The team at Empire Talent, especially Daryl Talbot and Kristen Maher for all their hard work.

The teams at Optus and Invisalign for all their support.

The team at Mont Adventure Equipment for providing all my gear needs, in particular David Edwards.

3 Degrees Marketing, especially my friend David Abela, Alex Rutman and Katelyn Flood.

All my teachers at Haileybury College, for being so flexible in accommodating my 'extra-curricular activites' outside school and who gave up their personal time to help me catch up on my missed schoolwork.

Leigh Gant at Op Meta for years of his strength and conditioning coaching and programming.

Dean Staples and Lydia Brady for their patient and caring guidance at the start of my journeys.

Jon Yeo from TEDx for teaching me how to talk on stage and share my message.

Michel, the French chef at the ALE South Pole camp for making me that ham and cheese sandwich.

Danielle Miller from Enlighten Education for all her encouragement and support early on in my journeys.

Everyone who posted messages of support on social media and online. We may not have met, but your positivity made an impact.

And last, but definitely not least, to the amazing team at Pan Macmillan for making this book a reality and truly caring about ensuring it tells my story in my own way – thank you to Claire Craig, Charlotte Ree, Danielle Walker and Carrie Hutchinson.

My family at the summit of Mt Kosciuszko
when I was six and Kane was four.

My best friends, Zoe (left) and Mia (right), and me
just before I flew out to Antarctica.

Heath (left), Ming (right) and me at the South Pole.

Villa and me celebrating my 16th birthday at The Blue Lagoon, Iceland.

Petter Nyquist and me in the Russian helicopter, North Pole 2016.